# Labor Arbitration– What you need to know

by Robert Coulson
President
American Arbitration
Association

REVISED THIRD EDITION

Third Edition, Revised January 1988


For information, write to
American Arbitration Association,
140 West 51st Street, New York, N.Y. 10020-1203
Library of Congress Catalog Card Number: 81-66912
ISBN 0-943001-05-6


First Printing, May 1981
Second Printing, August 1983
Third Printing, August 1986
Fourth Printing, January 1988
Fifth Printing, November 1990

# TABLE
# OF
# CONTENTS

# INTRODUCTION

## American
## Arbitration
## Association

The American Arbitration Association (AAA) is a public-service membership organization, founded in 1926 to encourage the use of arbitration and other techniques of voluntary dispute settlement. Members include companies, labor unions, law firms, foundations, and individuals who believe in alternative dispute resolution. The Association has become a national center of education, training, and research on all forms of out-of-court dispute settlement. Under its auspices, hundreds of educational programs are presented each year.

The AAA publishes three monthly labor arbitration award-reporting services; the quarterly *Arbitration Journal*; a quarterly legal letter; a quarterly newspaper, *Arbitration Times*; specialized pamphlets covering many fields of dispute resolution; and outlines for teaching labor relations and arbitration law courses. Among the materials produced by the Association are labor arbitration films and videotapes, each dealing with a typical grievance and illustrating procedures for resolving the dispute under AAA rules.

Arbitration is a useful institution. It affords labor unions an opportunity to provide an important advocacy service to their members. The grievance process keeps contract-interpretation questions out of the courts. Management knows that arbitration is preferable to work stoppage. American unions have learned that they do not have to strike over individual grievances. Compliance by both parties to the contract is assured. The arbitration of grievances is good business practice for both parties.

Arbitration is being used to resolve tens of thousands of disputes that unions and employers have been unable to settle through their grievance procedures. It permits the parties to test their positions against the judgment of an impartial arbitrator. It is a process that the parties have selected mutually. In its design and in its administration, the parties can exert control.

A healthy grievance procedure has a positive effect on the way labor and management get along in their day-to-day relations. Arbitration is more than a mechanism for coping with existing problems: it is a moral force, encouraging a spirit of cooperation that makes it possible for companies and unions to resolve problems without the agony of an adversarial process. The availability of a credible arbitration procedure ensures that both parties will be motivated to settle grievances amicably. This book is dedicated to the proposition that the highest calling of mankind is the task of bringing peace and understanding to the human condition.

Arbitration is serving an important function not only in labor relations: it is used to resolve a wide variety of business and community disputes. Millions of business contracts—construction, purchase and sale, leases, license agreements, franchises, and others—contain AAA arbitration clauses. Systems based upon traditional labor relations models are also found in agreements involving neighborhoods, student–faculty organizations, and other institutions. Here, too, the American Arbitration Association is playing a leading role.

# WHAT
# THIS BOOK
# CONTAINS

This book describes the process of labor arbitration. Its aim is to be helpful to anyone involved in a labor arbitration case. Whether you represent labor or management, you will be more effective if you understand how arbitration works and how you can make it work for you. The emphasis here will be on the practical.

The practice of labor arbitration has tended to become more uniform in recent years. Hearing procedures are, to a large degree, patterned on the Voluntary Labor Arbitration Rules of the American Arbitration Association. This book tells how to proceed under these rules. It contains practical advice to parties, based on the AAA's experience in administering more than 100,000 labor cases. The Voluntary Labor Arbitration Rules are printed in full, as are the Streamlined Labor Arbitration Rules, which provide a "fast-track" service for appropriate cases.

The AAA encourages parties to use arbitration as a problem-solving technique. This makes sense for both sides. Labor arbitration can be prompt and inexpensive. This handbook explains how parties can reduce cost and delay in their arbitration cases. Your primary interest may be how to win your case, but both parties have an interest in using arbitration constructively, to eliminate unnecessary conflict. A spirit of cooperation between management and the workforce is more important than victories in individual cases.

An important chapter describes some of the factors that should be considered when selecting an arbitrator. The selection procedure may vary, depending on the language of the arbitration clause in the contract and the wishes of the parties, but certain criteria should always be kept in mind. Nothing is more critical for your case than choosing the right arbitrator.

The ethical standards of labor arbitrators have consistently been high. To further encourage good practices, however, the Code of Professional Responsibility for Arbitrators of Labor–Management Disputes is reprinted in the appendix of this book. It has been approved by the AAA, the National Academy of Arbitrators, and the Federal Mediation and Conciliation Service.

Every activity accumulates its own jargon. Labor arbitration, too, requires an understanding of some basic technical words. The appendix contains a glossary of terms. To clarify the legal background of labor arbitration, the leading court cases on dispute resolution are described, and the text of the United States Arbitration Act is reprinted in full.

Since 1959, the American Arbitration Association has published a monthly *Summary of Labor Arbitration Awards*. This basic publication is supplemented with two specialized public-sector summaries, *Arbitration in the Schools* and *Labor Arbitration in Government*. As a by-product of these publications, the AAA has compiled a comprehensive index of the issues that have been resolved in labor arbitration cases. Also included in this book is a bibliography of arbitration literature prepared by the staff of the Lucius R. Eastman Arbitration Library.

The book you are reading is one you might want to have in your hip pocket when you discuss a grievance, participate in grievance procedures, or present an arbitration case. If you follow the suggestions in this book, you will be more likely to settle cases and to win those cases that cannot be settled.

If further information is needed about labor arbitration, inquiries can be directed to any AAA regional office. A list of these offices can be found at the end of this book. The AAA's regional staff help people to use alternative dispute resolution, providing advice and information about procedures and individual arbitrators.

Books, pamphlets, films, and videotapes on arbitration are also available from the AAA. Speakers and complete educational packages can be provided through the AAA's Department of Education and Training in New York City and Chicago.

Individuals or organizations interested in current information on labor arbitration can subscribe to particular services or become dues-paying AAA members. The AAA is a not-for-profit, public-service organization created to help parties resolve their disputes through voluntary, nongovernmental methods. Members have first call on all AAA research services, receive many regular publications, and get books, films, and training programs at a discount.

# CHAPTER 1

# SO YOU HAVE A LABOR GRIEVANCE

In labor relations, grievance arbitration has become an integral part of the labor contract. It was relatively easy to persuade private employers that binding arbitration was a better way to settle grievances than through strikes. That was good management.

Taft–Hartley and favorable court decisions helped to establish arbitration as the primary American grievance system. Grievance arbitration is recognized as an important American innovation, eliminating strikes and providing a mechanism through which unions can obtain realistic results from employment disputes. It has accomplished this without burdening the courts or regulatory agencies. In recent years, grievance arbitration has also been used in the public sector to resolve the problems of teachers, police officers, municipal clerks, and firefighters.

Millions of Americans participate in these procedures as grievants, witnesses, advocates, arbitrators, or persons affected by the decisions. Whether they are on the side of labor or management or serve as impartials, they need to understand the process. A few advocates and arbitrators specialize in labor arbitration, but most participants seldom arbitrate. When they do, they need to refresh their knowledge of the fundamentals. This book seeks to help such people by bringing them up to date.

Each grievance is unique. Depending upon the language of the particular collective bargaining contract, past practices between the parties, and their present relationship, the facts of each case will be different. Some situations may be relatively unimportant to the union or to the employer. Other grievances may probe vital interests of the parties, threatening important rights of individual employees, the profitability or even the existence of a company, or a union's power to represent its workers. Being a system created by people, the grievance and arbitration process displays all of the foibles of the individuals involved. The variety of potential human conflict lends drama to the practice and handling of these hundreds of thousands of industrial grievances.

In spite of such differences, there are common threads running through the grievance and arbitration practices of collective bargaining contracts. A description of customary practices will therefore be useful.

## READ YOUR GRIEVANCE PROCEDURE

The grievance and arbitration provisions of the collective bargaining agreement are interrelated. Only the hardiest grievances are likely to be arbitrated. Before the parties go to arbitration, the grievance will have endured a series of discussions and negotiations, during which both sides should have made a serious effort to resolve their problems. In a healthy relationship, fewer than 10 percent of the union's grievances have to go before an arbitrator for decision. If a higher percentage must be arbitrated, something could be wrong with the relationship. The parties should be concerned.

Union officials have an opportunity to screen out many cases. Some cases need never have been filed as grievances. Others can be withdrawn or settled. Losing an arbitration is a drain on the union: arbitration can be expensive, and a lost case reduces the union's credibility. Responsible restraint by the union will build a better batting average and best serve the interests of its members.

On the other hand, an analysis of the situation may indicate that employer representatives were inflexible in their handling of employee complaints. A harsh personnel policy will often generate unnecessary grievances.

Arbitration is only one of a number of alternatives that parties may use to resolve their disputes. In recent years, other forms of dispute resolution have become prevalent.

Mediation is an increasingly popular alternative dispute resolution technique. A mediator meets with the parties or their representatives, attempting to arrange an acceptable solution. A mediator has no authority to make decisions for the parties. Rather, a mediator helps them to analyze the issues and to exchange perceptions, seeking a formula for compromise. The experience thus far has been positive.

Where representatives of the parties are wasting too much time contesting grievances and processing labor arbitrations, joint discussions at a higher level might identify the reasons for the situation and resolve them. Help from a mediator can be useful in this effort.

There are many kinds of grievance procedures. Some are relatively simple, others far too complicated. You should read your contract carefully to determine whether the grievance procedure is appropriate for your needs. Each step should be appraised, particularly for how it has worked in practice.

Does each step resolve a reasonable percentage of grievances? Is the procedure self-executing? The moving party should be able to count on the various steps taking place without having to go to court. The grievance and arbitration procedure in the collective bargaining contract is intended to avoid the need for litigation, with its delays, expense, and anxieties. Its purpose is to enforce the contractual obligations of the parties, establishing employment conditions consistent with the terms of the collective bargaining agreement. That is why it makes sense to provide for an administrative agency to make procedural decisions. Only a small percentage of labor grievances result in any kind of litigation. Court cases are the exception, a sign of failure.

At the same time, the grievance procedure should be recognized as an adversarial process. Some conflict is inevitable in a complex, changing relationship. The challenge to both parties is to develop systems for the creative management of industrial conflict.

## THE LANGUAGE OF THE CONTRACT

Parties should be certain that the grievance system is tailored to their needs. It may take many forms. Both parties should satisfy themselves that their own arrangement is rational and appropriate.

The arbitration provision should also be reviewed. Does the arbitration clause give the moving party the unilateral right to initiate the grievance and place it before an arbitrator? Or can procedural impasses force the parties into court? Thousands of labor arbitration clauses refer to the American Arbitration Association. Untested clauses can be defective, offering ample opportunity to disrupt the procedure. How about yours?

By referring to the AAA as their administrative agency, parties can protect themselves — provided the AAA is authorized to do more than merely appoint an arbitrator. If one of the parties refuses to arbitrate, the use of the AAA's Voluntary Labor Arbitration Rules guarantees that the grievance can still be placed before an arbitrator. Under section 12 of the rules, for example, the AAA is authorized to appoint an arbitrator if the parties are unable to agree on one. If it is impossible for the parties to arrange a hearing date, the arbitrator can fix a time and place for the hearing under rule 19. There is no need for delay after the hearing. Under rule 37, the arbitrator must render the award within 30 days after the hearing is closed. If the arbitrator needs more time, the AAA will seek a waiver from both parties. A system of arbitration that is quick, economical, and effective can be an important benefit to both parties. Such a system can be obtained by providing in the contract for AAA administration.

Arbitration agreements often represent a compromise based upon the parties' relative bargaining strengths, political considerations, and other practical needs. The practical experience of negotiators may be reflected in the procedure. This is not always the case: arbitration clauses are sometimes scribbled into the contract in the final rush of bargaining. Beware! The grievance and arbitration provisions are vital parts of the bargaining procedure. They should be designed with care.

Arbitration is most often used to enforce the rights of union members, but either party may feel a need to clarify the meaning and application of the contract. The arbitration clause then becomes the mechanism under which a matter can be submitted to an impartial expert for a mutually binding decision.

The arbitration clause has an impact upon the parties' behavior. Management actions affecting the interests of union members are responsive to the union's right to arbitrate. Under some clauses, union actions contested by the employer may also be subject to arbitration. The availability of arbitration has a tendency to direct the actions of both parties toward fairness and accountability. The arbitration clause creates "contractual responsibility" between the parties. It forces both parties to abide by contract obligations in a spirit of mutual self-regulation.

## ARBITRATION IS PARTICIPATION

The grievance and arbitration process requires the involvement of many persons throughout an organization. It is a participatory system. As a result, training and orientation are needed so that everyone can understand and make the best use of the system. Not only must the official representatives of the parties be well versed as to their rights and obligations under the contract, they must also be able to explain those rights and obligations to their associates, including how to use the grievance and arbitration system. Training in case preparation and advocacy is needed.

Management organizations and unions can obtain advocacy training for their own representatives. In addition, the AAA conducts dispute resolution seminars during which representatives of labor and management are exposed to the thinking of experienced labor arbitrators. Hearing procedures, arbitrability, such substantive issues as discipline, discharge, management rights, and seniority, and other practical problems are discussed by experts. The AAA also offers participants an opportunity to practice their skills in mock proceedings.

Some union and employer representatives are inexperienced in presenting cases in arbitration. Much can be done to sharpen their skills. The Department of Education and Training of the American Arbitration Association is a resource for those who wish to learn more about how labor arbitration can be used efficiently. Labor arbitration seminars of all kinds are available. If your clients or associates need this kind of training, contact an AAA Regional Office or the AAA Department of Education and Training. We would be glad to include them in seminars, providing an opportunity to meet and exchange views with practitioners from both union and employer groups. Shared experience can be put to good use. By participating in mock hearings, participants can better understand the purpose and techniques of labor arbitration.

The American Arbitration Association produces a wide variety of training materials, including pamphlets of basic instruction and training films and videotapes. You should take advantage of these materials.

I recommend that organizations not limit such training to the advocates who actually represent clients at arbitrations: other people involved in grievance discussions should be included. Labor arbitration is participatory. Many people can contribute to the discussions. Each one should understand how labor arbitration works and how a case should be presented. The American Arbitration Association is an impartial organization seeking to make arbitration work efficiently for both parties.

It is important to create a positive approach. Here, the responsibility shifts to the top leadership of the organizations involved. Arbitration can be used as a problem solver, but it can also be abused. Unnecessary grievances should not be permitted to clog the arbitration process. Nor should the parties be denied a fair hearing. By acting responsibly, parties can avoid having to take their disputes to court. Labor arbitration should not be total war, even though it is an adversarial process. Maintaining a healthy relationship between the parties is often more important than winning a particular case.


## MAKING GRIEVANCE ARBITRATION WORK FOR BOTH PARTIES


In the United States, collective bargaining has flourished as a method for working out the arrangements of labor unions, on behalf of the workers they represent, and of management, on behalf of the other participants in the enterprise. National labor laws have encouraged this process. For settling disputes over the interpretation or application of collective bargaining agreements, unions and employers have been persuaded to create mutually acceptable procedures, which have usually taken the form of joint grievance discussions terminating in arbitration.

Grievance and arbitration procedures are found in most collective bargaining contracts. Hundreds of thousands of labor disputes concerning the contract rights of union workers have been resolved in this way without government intervention.

Collective bargaining is well established. Labor arbitration is the instrument of choice for resolving labor grievances. In recent years, however, some systems have become bogged down in legal procedures.

There are other symptoms of distress. Discontent has been expressed by some union members about the costs and delays of their system of arbitration. Critical articles have appeared. Is the labor arbitration mill grinding too slowly? Is arbitration becoming too expensive? Is the system really responsive to the needs of the individual worker?

As an impartial agency, the AAA encourages parties to help make arbitration work more efficiently and at less cost. We want the process to be fair.

If parties would exercise restraint in bringing grievances to arbitration, substantial savings could be achieved. Many cases are arbitrated unnecessarily; union representatives must try harder to screen out the "losers." The AAA's filing fee may encourage union officials to exercise this responsibility. Only bona fide cases are likely to be filed where a fee is charged. In the long run, charging a fee to each party benefits unions as well as employers. No one's interest is served by the filing of an unnecessary claim. Under some arbitration systems, grievances are filed without any expectation that they will ever be heard by an arbitrator. This is less likely under AAA procedures. More than 80 percent of the cases filed with the AAA actually proceed to the appointment of an arbitrator.

An arbitrator will follow whatever procedure is selected by the parties. It is the parties' responsibility to adopt sensible administrative practices. They should look for

21

ways to improve their system. Both unions and employers have an interest in expediting their grievance and arbitration machinery. They should not permit their representatives to load arbitration with unnecessary costs or inappropriate procedural steps.

Here are some points to bear in mind.

## STIPULATIONS

One way to reduce delay in the arbitration process is to agree on the issues in advance. Time is often wasted at hearings because the representatives of the parties have failed to do this. In some cases, parties will find it helpful to sit down with an AAA administrator prior to the hearing, in an effort to agree on an agenda. Some issues can be stipulated, and arrangements can be made for presenting evidence in an orderly fashion.

## DOING WITHOUT A TRANSCRIPT

Although arrangements for transcripts can be made by the parties, they should be ordered only reluctantly. Not only are transcripts expensive, but they contribute in a number of secondary ways to the cost and delay of the process. Where one party requests a transcript, the other may assume that it needs one as well. The arbitrator may then feel obliged to refer to it in preparing the opinion. The availability of a transcript increases the likelihood that the parties will file posthearing briefs.

In any case, preparation of a transcript takes time. Reading a transcript takes time. Briefs take time. Transcripts are one of the prime sources of delay and cost in the arbitration process. Whenever possible, the parties should eliminate transcripts from the procedure.

As an alternative, some parties have been using tape recorders to make a record of the hearing for their own purposes. Some labor arbitrators use recorders to supplement their own notes. The tape does not become the official record of the hearing, but it can be useful for recalling points that were made or testimony that was introduced.

In a few cases, an official record of the hearing will be necessary. Where the arbitration award might later be reviewed by the NLRB or by a court, for example, a transcript can show what evidence was considered by the arbitrator in reaching the decision. Even in those cases, however, a comprehensive opinion from the arbitrator can serve the same purpose.

## WAIVING OF BRIEFS

Briefs also are sometimes necessary. But parties should remember that a brief will require that the arbitrator spend additional study time.

In a few cases, a prehearing memorandum can help focus the arbitrator's attention upon the issues. In other situations, the same information can be presented orally.

It is not customary for labor arbitrators to be exposed to the case before they appear at the hearing. Both parties have an equal opportunity to make their oral presentations to the best of their ability. Some prefer to provide the arbitrator with a prearbitration statement of the case.

A posthearing brief is more common in labor arbitration, particularly where one or both parties are represented by lawyers. Parties should discuss with their attorneys the necessity of such a brief. Unless there are complex legal issues involved, the closing statement made at the end of the case is enough to set the issues before the arbitrator. If briefs are filed, additional study time will be required. Not only must the arbitrator read the briefs, but testimony and arguments might fade from memory while the briefs are being prepared. In some cases, such delay can actually diminish the impact of the parties' presentations.

## ASKING FOR A PROMPT DECISION

The parties can request an arbitrator to render an immediate decision—to prepare an award on the spot, followed by a summary opinion. Under the AAA's expedited sets of rules, the arbitrator is given a few days to write a summary opinion. In many cases, this is all the parties need to resolve their problem. Sometimes no written opinion will be necessary; the decision itself may be enough.

An arbitrator charges for both the days of the hearing and for time spent preparing an opinion. By eliminating the need for an elaborate opinion, parties can reduce the total cost of arbitration. In other situations, the parties can sharply reduce the arbitrator's total fee by not citing cases in their closing statements or posthearing briefs.

Parties are not always enthusiastic about saving time and money in the arbitration process. Attorneys may be even less concerned. But neither party is served if delay causes employees to become disenchanted with the system. Both sides have a practical interest in expediting the procedure.

Arbitration can perform only as well as the parties permit. Both the union and the employer should try to make arbitration work in accordance with the needs and desires of the workers. The frustrations created by a congested arbitration system tend to poison the employment relationship. The AAA feels justified in calling upon both sides to exercise responsible restraint.

## STREAMLINED ARBITRATION RULES

All of the time and cost savers described above are incorporated into the AAA's Streamlined Labor Arbitration Rules, which are included in the Voluntary Labor Arbitration Rules. These rules appear in the appendix. Grievances can be submitted to arbitration under these rules, if both parties agree.

Under these rules, hearings are scheduled within seven days of the appointment of an arbitrator. Unless the parties agree otherwise, there are no transcripts or briefs. In conventional arbitration, the parties have seven days to select an arbitrator. In an expedited procedure, they give the AAA the power to appoint an arbitrator. In practice, the regional office generally calls the parties with the names of a few arbitrators who are available to serve on short notice, attempting to make a mutually acceptable appointment. The rules provide for a single hearing. The award is due within five business days after the hearing.

## THE COST OF ARBITRATION

The cost of arbitration can be a problem. There are practical ways to reduce this cost.

1. One expense is clearly within the control of each party—the time and money spent by the parties and their representatives in investigating facts and preparing exhibits. Streamlining this process reduces the costs.

In complex cases, parties sometimes require the help of outside experts, such as economists or time-study engineers. Such expenditures are not necessary in most grievance arbitrations. Very often, by stipulating some of the facts, a party can substantially reduce the cost of preparation.

2. Another item of expense, the stenographic record, can easily be avoided. As a general rule, arbitrators take their own notes; a transcript is optional for the parties. In particularly complicated cases, stenographic records may be requested by the arbitrator. Transcripts may also be necessary for parties in the preparation of briefs. But in most cases the transcript can be eliminated.

As was pointed out earlier, a tape recorder can be used to refresh one's memory of a case. The quality of such equipment has improved tremendously in recent years. Many arbitrators are using portable recorders.

A party who does require a stenographic record should arrange to have a reporter present at hearings. The party or parties ordering the record are billed directly by the reporting agency.

3. The third item of expense is the fee of the arbitrator. These charges usually range from $250 to $650 per day of hearing and study time required for the preparation of the award. On average, 1.4 days of study time are charged for each day of hearing. Under AAA practice, the rate

of compensation is agreed upon in advance. Along with the arbitrator's fee, there may be reimbursement for travel, accommodations, and incidental costs. Sometimes parties use the services of distant arbitrators rather than equally qualified arbitrators from their own area. Why? There are good arbitrators in every part of the country. The regional AAA administrator knows who they are and whether they are available.

Parties should recognize that briefs, transcripts, case citations, and multiple hearings will add to the arbitrator's fee and thus increase the cost of the proceedings.

4. The fourth item is the fee that each party pays to the AAA. For this, the AAA performs the administrative work in connection with the selection of the arbitrator, the scheduling of hearings, and the general supervision of the case. The participation of the AAA expedites the case, usually resulting in substantial savings and guarding against procedural impasses that might otherwise require resort to the courts.

## EXPEDITED ARBITRATION IN THE PUBLIC SECTOR

Simplification is particularly appropriate in the public sector, where there are many small bargaining units and employers. There is no need to waste union dues or tax-payers' money on complicated and expensive procedures. AAA regional vice presidents can help. When a union files a case, it can indicate whether the parties will agree on an expedited procedure. We are glad to help parties eliminate unnecessary procedural problems.

When appropriate, unions and employers should handle most of their grievance arbitration cases on an expedited basis. Does a simple question of discipline require the full treatment of transcripts, briefs, and a lengthy opinion? A simple oral hearing should be held before an arbitrator. Expensive briefs should be eliminated. The arbitrator can be asked to write a summary opinion, to be delivered soon after the hearing. Streamlined arbitration is in everyone's interest.

## ARBITRATORS' FEES

While there has been a modest rise in per diem rates, only part of the increase in labor arbitration costs can be traced to arbitrators' fees. AAA statistics disclose that arbitrators have been charging less study time on AAA cases. In recent years, the ratio between hearing days and study days has declined.

Although arbitrators' fees have risen, the increase is substantially less than the increase in fees of most other professionals.

Labor arbitrators are aware of the need to charge reasonable fees. Arbitration is a unique profession: after the case, the arbitrator must collect half of the fee from each party. Losing parties are not likely to show gratitude to an arbitrator who held against them. If arbitrators were charging unreasonable fees, they would have difficulty collecting them; but this is seldom the case.

Parties should be sure that time is being spent productively during the processing of the case. Hearings should begin promptly in the morning and continue throughout the day, with a short break for lunch. Wherever possible, the matter should be completed at the first hearing. Most labor arbitrators are willing to stay late to avoid the need for a subsequent session.

## POSITIVE APPROACH TO ARBITRATION

Used intelligently and prudently, arbitration will continue to be an effective part of the collective bargaining contract. Not only will it resolve disputes, but it will help communication between union leadership and management and between employees and employer.

Many years of administrative experience in the labor arbitration field, during which tens of thousands of labor cases have been administered, have convinced the American Arbitration Association that parties should control their own practices.

It is not difficult to design and administer an effective grievance procedure. Many parties have done so. Informality was the original concept: grievances would be handled quickly and economically. If the parties want such a procedure, they have only to ask for it.

In most labor relations settings, grievance arbitration is healthy and serviceable; but where breakdowns occur, they tend to discredit the entire institution. They instill discontent among the rank-and-file union members, who generalize from the particular and reject the entire concept.

Too many parties permit unnecessary delays and expenses — multiple steps in the grievance procedure, formality, briefs and transcripts adding to the cost, long-winded arguments about arbitrability, attempts to keep out evidence, and adjournments and postponements — for reasons that often relate more to convenience than to the merits of the case. These procedures can impede the arbitration.

Every collective bargaining contract should be reviewed by the parties to scrutinize the administration of the procedure for bottlenecks and to encourage expedition. The system should be looked at through the eyes of the individual grievants who must live with the procedure.

It should not be too difficult to identify the problems that are responsible for employee discontent. The system should be analyzed. What are the reasons for delay and for unreasonable costs? How could cases be expedited? Which steps could be eliminated?

This is not an academic exercise for labor unions. With the surge of fair representation cases in recent years, the union must protect itself by providing an efficient grievance system for its members. Union members expect arbitration to be a swift and rational avenue of justice. Members become frustrated, alienated, and bitter when they are faced with unexplained delays, where legal mumbo-jumbo keeps them from telling their story.

Although labor arbitration has some problems, it is working well. It serves its purpose, solving problems for union leaders and for executives. In hundreds of thousands of contractual relationships, the grievance and arbitration system is quietly going about its business, helping parties to settle their disagreements.

# CHAPTER 2

# HOW TO SELECT A LABOR ARBITRATOR

Arbitrators are chosen in various ways. Many contracts contain a reference to the Voluntary Labor Arbitration Rules of the American Arbitration Association. This chapter describes how arbitrators are chosen under that system.

No part of the arbitration clause is more important than how the arbitrator will be selected. The predictability of arbitration depends substantially upon the knowledge, experience, and understanding that the arbitrator brings to the hearing.

A survey of AAA cases indicates that many local unions and employers have only one or two arbitrations a year. Representatives of such parties might be unfamiliar with the relative abilities of individual arbitrators. In contrast, other practitioners use labor arbitration constantly and come to know the arbitrators very well. A selection process that is appropriate for the experienced labor lawyer might not meet the needs of the novice.

The tripartite system, once popular, now seems unnecessarily complicated. In labor arbitration, the so-called party-appointed arbitrator is merely an advocate. Most parties prefer a system in which the case is presented to one impartial arbitrator. That way, everything is in the open. Employees tend to distrust tripartite panels, suspecting that deals and compromises take place. The trend in grievance arbitration is toward one neutral arbitrator.

Careful consideration should be given to the selection process set forth in the collective bargaining agreement. Most labor arbitration provisions guarantee parties the right to participate in the selection of an arbitrator. The facts and circumstances of the case and full information about available arbitrators should be carefully appraised by the parties before a selection is made. This process should result in an appointment of the best available arbitrator. It is here that the *ad hoc* system displays its strength.

A technique for suggesting appropriate names to parties in connection with specific cases is contained in the AAA Voluntary Labor Arbitration Rules. This system relies heavily upon the judgment of the AAA's tribunal administrators. As the New York State Supreme Court has stated, "The AAA, through a long and active career, has gained an enviable reputation for the absolute impartiality of its conduct in all the various steps and phases of arbitration—so much so that it is commonly designated by the parties in contracts providing for arbitration."

AAA regional vice presidents and their staff keep abreast of qualified labor arbitrators in their own area. They know which arbitrators are available and what kind of cases they are best suited to handle. If parties require an arbitrator with special expertise, the regional office will recognize these differences in submitting a list of arbitrators. A small union arbitrating a discipline case against a local job-shop may need a list of arbitrators quite different from the list provided when a large union brings a more complicated case against a national manufacturer.

Some contracts do not specify how the parties are to select an arbitrator. A list can always be obtained from the AAA. At any stage, parties to a labor dispute can turn to the AAA for help. If the AAA is specified in the collective bargaining contract, the procedure is automatic.

## SELECTING THE ARBITRATOR
## UNDER AAA PROCEDURES

Unless parties have selected a different method, the American Arbitration Association's procedure is as follows:

1. Upon receiving a demand for arbitration, the AAA acknowledges receipt and sends each party a copy of a specially prepared list of proposed arbitrators. In drawing up this list, the tribunal administrator will be guided primarily by the nature of the dispute. Basic information about each arbitrator is attached to the list. Where parties need more information about a proposed arbitrator, the AAA is glad to supply it by telephone.

2. The parties cross off unacceptable names and state their order of preference as to those remaining. If they prefer, they may alternate in striking names from a list.

3. When the lists are returned by the parties, the AAA determines which of the arbitrators is most acceptable. That arbitrator is then contacted. The arbitrator is asked to supply available dates and whether there is any reason why he or she could not act with impartiality in a dispute

between the parties. The Code of Professional Responsibility included in this book serves as a guide for arbitrators as to what should be disclosed.

4. Where parties are unable to reach a mutual choice from a list, the AAA will submit additional lists, but only at the request of both sides. If the parties still fail to agree upon an arbitrator, the AAA is authorized to make an administrative appointment. In no case, however, will an arbitrator be appointed whose name was crossed off by either party.

Collective bargaining agreements sometimes provide for tripartite arbitration boards without setting time limits for appointment of the party-appointed arbitrators. Even there, the AAA system can give force and effect to the wishes of the parties.

Where the agreement provides for selection of the third, impartial member of a board "by the American Arbitration Association," lists are sent to the parties or to the party-appointed arbitrators, in accordance with the terms of the contract or the wishes of the parties.

## ARBITRATOR LISTS

The AAA submits lists in accordance with the particular arbitration clause involved. In addition, the list reflects what is known about the past preferences of the parties. The regional office knows that its performance will be judged by the quality of the lists it issues.

The AAA serves as a facilitating agency, seeking to foresee which arbitrators will be acceptable to both parties.

By having this judgment made by a local representative, sensitive and informed service can be provided.

After the AAA supplies the list, the responsibility for the selection process shifts to the advocates. What do parties need to know about a particular arbitrator? What useful information can the AAA supply? What must be obtained elsewhere?

## SOURCES OF INFORMATION

A copy of each arbitrator's biography is mailed out with the list being submitted. Each AAA office is prepared to provide parties with additions and updates, as needed. Parties may wish to study recent awards that the arbitrators have rendered, particularly on similar issues.

The AAA's monthly *Summary of Labor Arbitration Awards* has reported many thousands of decisions since its inception in April 1959. The issues considered, the names of the arbitrator and the parties, and the location of the hearing are included in each summary.

This service can be especially useful to a party wishing to find out what particular arbitrators have previously written on similar issues. The cumulative index enables their decisions to be easily located. The full text of opinions that are of interest can then be obtained directly from the AAA.

Similar summaries are published for arbitration cases in the public sector. These are *Arbitration in the Schools* and *Labor Arbitration in Government*. In addition, the AAA maintains an award bank that contains thousands of unpublished opinions, rendered by AAA arbitrators or sent in by arbitrators to provide samples of their work.

## COMMERCIAL SERVICES AND
## OTHER SOURCES

Other publishers also report arbitration awards, and awards rendered by permanent umpires are published as well. Several commercial services, catering to management, report the opinions of employers and their counsel who have used a particular arbitrator in prior cases. Subscribers receive such information by paying an annual fee.

Management groups maintain information about arbitrators, as do several of the management-oriented law firms. When a member of the network uses an arbitrator, he or she is asked to fill out a report form which becomes part of the material on file.

In the same way, unions and labor-oriented law firms collect similar information available to union officials. These networks are sometimes administered by education directors of the international unions.

Practitioners search out networks of information available for their use. There are ways to find out what the people on your side of the bargaining table think of a particular arbitrator.

## EVALUATING AN ARBITRATOR

Information about a particular arbitrator can be obtained from parties who have used that arbitrator on prior cases. What do they say about the arbitrator's ability, philosophy, and impartiality? Can the arbitrator understand the particular kinds of issues that are involved in the case? Does the arbitrator have the competence to sift facts in an adversarial proceeding? Does the arbitrator have the engineering or technical background required on certain issues or experience in the particular industry? Is the arbitrator too legalistic or not legalistic enough? Is the individual's particular philosophy suitable for the issues of the case? These are some of the questions that will be asked about the arbitrator being selected. Parties interested in winning their case can try to forecast the arbitrator's reaction.

Evaluating an arbitrator is a matter of opinion, which varies from advocate to advocate. Many practitioners believe that their experience makes it possible for them to match each issue to an arbitrator. By learning where to turn for information about arbitrators, the practitioner can do a better job of selecting the right arbitrator for the case. Nothing in labor arbitration is more important.

## USING THE MORE AVAILABLE ARBITRATORS

One unfortunate by-product of the system is that practitioners become hesitant to accept an unknown quantity. The tried-and-true arbitrators are used again and again, and the new, but fully qualified, arbitrator may not get chosen.

Introducing relatively unknown arbitrators into the process is not easy, although the situation is not as hopeless as is sometimes claimed. New men and women coming into the profession are now being accepted, some with surprising speed. More than one hundred new arbitrators obtain appointments each year.

The conservatism of advocates reflects pressure placed upon union agents and company personnel to select arbitrators who will render acceptable awards. The unknown quantity of a relatively new arbitrator is particularly frightening to a person who is under such pressure. It is advisable, however, for parties to permit their representatives to take a chance on new arbitrators in appropriate cases.

Many qualified arbitrators are available. For its part, the American Arbitration Association seeks out arbitrators already on the panel who are being underutilized, considering their experience and potential acceptability. In addition, it continues to train new labor arbitrators to enter the field. The AAA also attempts to increase their visibility by sponsoring labor-management conferences where new arbitrators can meet practitioners and by publishing awards by new arbitrators in its monthly services. Parties, for their part, are encouraged to select arbitrators who are new or underutilized. In the long run, they will benefit by having a larger pool of arbitrators.

## INTRODUCING NEW ARBITRATORS TO THE LABOR-MANAGEMENT COMMUNITY

What can a new labor arbitrator do to become more widely accepted in the profession? An arbitrator must be able to perform competently. Beyond this, an arbitrator needs to be favorably known on a personal basis throughout the labor-management community. If possible, an arbitrator should join appropriate professional groups. It helps to publish articles in *The Arbitration Journal* and other recognized publications.

We asked a number of newly successful arbitrators how they gained acceptability. This is what they said:

- Meet other arbitrators and lawyers at bar association meetings. Attempt to become listed by state agencies.

- Get to know the local groups of labor lawyers through meetings of the Industrial Relations Research Association (IRRA), Society of Professionals in Dispute Resolution (SPIDR), and other organizations.

- Become known to the parties on a personal and professional basis. Participate in and attend conferences and education programs.

- Audit arbitral hearings with accepted arbitrators to provide personal contacts with both parties. Parties may not select a neutral that they have not had a chance to meet.

- Be professional, both in the conduct of hearings and in the writing of opinions and awards.

- Run hearings effectively and spend a lot of time on early awards, without billing for the full time spent on preparation.

- Attend sessions scheduled by the AAA where parties and arbitrators meet.

- Look for internships, which are a good way to break in but are hard to find.

- Be well versed in the field of collective bargaining. Learn federal and state labor laws.

- Serve as a neutral in mediation and gain the trust and confidence of the parties.

- Serve an apprenticeship with a busy arbitrator.

- Serve as an *ad hoc* factfinder or mediator. Make contacts with labor and management representatives and neutrals through such organizations as IRRA and SPIDR.

- Acquire training and experience in the labor relations field; demonstrate an active and sincere interest in being an arbitrator; write well-reasoned, concise, and timely opinions when selected.

- Donate time to voluntary work in all industrial relations areas, such as schools, committees, and speaking engagements.

- Meet the people who appoint arbitrators. Complete a comprehensive training course.

- Gain exposure in nonarbitral settings. When selected for the first few cases, be firm, courteous, and demonstrate knowledge, understanding, and integrity. Permit full development of the parties' cases. Write up the parties' arguments fully and persuasively, whether they win or lose.

- Before becoming an active candidate, obtain maximum experience in labor relations with either management or unions. Thereafter, pursue activity in professional organizations.

- Gain initial experience as an advocate in labor relations. Work in the personnel department for either a company or a labor organization.

• Study the literature intensively, so the initial cases will be well handled.

• Make availability known to practitioners who are in a position to select an arbitrator. Become a member on all possible arbitrator panels. In addition to AAA and FMCS, state and local agencies use mediators and fact-finders. Any appointments of this nature can help one gain exposure and experience.

• Attend training sessions sponsored by various agencies.

## HOW ARBITRATORS GET ON THE AAA PANEL

The American Arbitration Association has created a roster of arbitrators for use in all kinds of labor arbitration cases throughout the country. Over 3,500 labor arbitrators are now on the panel, although most of the work is done by about 1,200 active arbitrators. Most labor arbitrators in the United States are on the AAA panel.

How are new persons appointed? How are candidates screened by the AAA? How is the quality of the panel maintained?

The AAA's officers and regional vice presidents search for people who have good potential for being accepted as labor arbitrators. Men and women selected on an *ad hoc* basis by parties in their local area are one source of talent. Some arbitrators come from government labor relations agencies. Still others teach industrial relations or labor law at universities or have a strong academic background in these fields. Attorneys and other professionals with a knowledge of industrial relations are frequently accepted.

A few experienced labor arbitrators also serve as advocates for labor or management. This usually reduces potential acceptability, unless offset by indications of acceptability through an established record of service as a neutral. Practicing advocates are therefore not encouraged to apply to the AAA national panel.

When a nomination is received from a reliable source, an invitation is issued. In some cases, an informal investigation indicates that it would be a waste of time to process the candidate's application. It serves no good purpose for an inexperienced or inappropriate person to apply.

Each applicant to the AAA's labor panel is required to pay a processing fee, which can be applied to membership in the AAA.

## LABOR PANEL DATA SHEET

The candidate is required to fill out a labor panel data sheet. This document has two parts. One requires information about the candidate, present and previous business affiliations, professional licenses, education, and previous employment. While most labor arbitrators have a thorough academic background, often including law school, a few have not completed such training. Most labor arbitrators have had some prior experience with practical industrial relations, but there are some who have never worked in the field. Many arbitrators are lawyers; almost one-third are not. Most lawyer arbitrators do not represent clients in labor relations, but some do. The guidelines are not rigid: exceptions are found to each general section.

The second part is also important. Each candidate is asked to give the names of four union, four management, and four neutral references who can comment on the candidate's character and abilities. Many of the references are positive, but some people say that they cannot recommend the person who used their name. Reading between the lines of a reference letter sometimes reveals a reservation about a candidate. A frank telephone call to its writer can clarify the problem. In about one-third of the cases, the reference letters will indicate a need for further investigation.

## ADMITTANCE TO THE PANEL

A candidate may be admitted to the panel on the basis of the application form and letters of reference. The decision to accept candidates is made administratively by AAA staff.

Within two weeks of acceptance to the labor panel, the new arbitrator's biographical information is entered into the AAA's computerized records. It includes a listing of current and previous full-time positions and the years involved as well as experience in labor relations with particular industries and issues. Contract arbitrator designation is also mentioned, along with the names of the employers, government agencies, or unions who have so designated the arbitrator. A card is generated and forwarded along with the completed file to the office covering the area where the arbitrator is located. In some instances, the card will be sent to two regional offices, one covering the business location and another covering the residential address (see pp. 175–176 for the locations of our regional offices). Once an arbitrator has demonstrated acceptability, in the arbitrator's local region (e.g., by rendering five awards there), listing in other regions is permitted.

Arbitrators sometimes lose their acceptability. Illness or advanced age may cause the arbitrator's judgment to be distrusted. Sometimes arbitrators encounter temporary personal problems, such as alcoholism, nervous breakdowns, or the like. These problems may require that the arbitrator's name not be submitted on lists. Where an arbitrator habitually overcharges parties, is unable to arrange a hearing within a reasonable time, or is consistently late in rendering awards, AAA offices may stop sending out that name on lists. Regional vice presidents will sometimes be advised to use an arbitrator with caution.

The AAA's primary responsibility is to provide parties with the best possible arbitrators. It relies heavily upon the judgment of its local regional vice presidents, who must weigh the acceptability of each arbitrator on their panel against the needs of the parties in the particular case. The regional office has responsibility for preparing lists for cases and for selecting the best names for the parties and the issues. Regional staff are expected to know their panel members' experience, expertise in special fields, availability for quick service, billing practices, and record of acceptability with particular companies and unions. This knowledge is of practical benefit when lists are issued on pending cases.

The AAA serves the labor–management community by maintaining an excellent list of arbitrators, by submitting carefully selected lists in accordance with the arbitration clause in each collective bargaining contract, and by introducing new arbitrators whenever the parties agree to use them.

# CHAPTER 3

# THE
# ARBITRATION
# HEARING

By the time a case reaches arbitration, representatives of both parties will have spent many hours discussing the grievance. In these talks, at each level of the grievance procedure, they have become familiar with all the facts and complications of the matter. If they are unable to settle the case, they will have to prepare themselves to present the facts to an arbitrator who knows nothing about the dispute until the hearing begins.

Effective presentation of the facts and arguments must begin with thorough preparation. The following steps are recommended:

1. Study the original statement of the grievance and review its history through every step of the grievance machinery.

2. Review the collective bargaining agreement. Clauses which at first glance seem unrelated to the grievance may often be found to have some bearing.

3. Assemble all documents and papers you will need at the hearing. Make photocopies for the arbitrator and

for the other party. If some of the documents you need are in the possession of the other party, ask that they be brought to the arbitration. The arbitrator usually has authority to subpoena documents and witnesses if they cannot be made available in any other way.

4. Interview all of your witnesses. Make certain they understand the theory of your case, as well as the importance of their own testimony. Run through the testimony several times. Rehearse the probable cross-examination.

5. Make a written summary of the testimony of each witness. This can be useful as a checklist at the hearing to ensure that nothing is overlooked.

6. Study the case from the other side's point of view. Be prepared for opposing evidence and arguments.

7. Discuss your outline of the case with others in your organization. A fresh viewpoint will often disclose weak spots that you may have overlooked.

8. Read published awards on the issues that seem to be involved in your case. While awards by other arbitrators on cases between other parties are not decisive as to your own case, they may be persuasive. The American Arbitration Association has published summaries of thousands of labor arbitration awards in its monthly publications. Use these summaries and their cumulative indexes as research tools.

# PRESENTATION OF THE ARBITRATION CASE

Arbitration hearings are less formal than court trials. The parties and their attorneys sit on opposite sides of a conference table; the arbitrator sits at the head. The hearing is orderly.

Arbitrators expect to hear all the evidence that is relevant and material to the issue. Because they must determine for themselves what is relevant, arbitrators are inclined to accept evidence that might not be allowed by judges. This does not mean, however, that all evidence is of equal weight or that irrelevant or repetitious evidence will not be rejected by the arbitrator. Arbitrators are not required to follow courtroom rules of evidence. In fact, they may lose patience with a party that keeps making technical objections.

Your evidence can often be established by documents and exhibits. Documentary evidence may be an essential part of the case. In some instances, key words, phrases, and sections of written documents should be highlighted to focus the arbitrator's attention on the essential part. Properly presented documentary evidence can be most persuasive and merits careful handling.

Direct testimony may be necessary. After a witness is identified and qualified, he or she should be allowed to testify largely without interruption. Although leading questions may be permitted in arbitration, testimony is more effective when the witness relates facts from knowledge. Questions from counsel may be useful in emphasizing the points being made.

# EVIDENCE AND PROOF

The arbitrator must provide a fair hearing, giving both parties sufficient opportunity to present their respective evidence and arguments. The AAA rules provide that "the Arbitrator shall be the judge of the relevance and materiality of the evidence offered and conformity to legal rules of evidence shall not be necessary."

There are many reasons why technical evidentiary rules are not suitable in arbitration. First, arbitration is intended to be an informal procedure. Second, the rules of evidence are essentially rules of exclusion. They were developed to prevent a jury from hearing or considering prejudicial or unreliable testimony and exhibits. In arbitration, a sophisticated person, selected by the parties for technical knowledge and good judgment, hears the case; such a person should be able to disregard evidence that is not helpful, relevant, or reliable. Third, there may be a therapeutic value in allowing the witnesses to vent their feelings or "get things off their chests," even if the testimony has little probative value. Finally, an award will not be overturned because of liberal admission of evidence as long as the arbitrator does not base the award on obviously irrelevant or erroneous evidence. On the other hand, refusal to hear relevant evidence may constitute grounds for vacating the award.

To say that conformity to the legal rules of evidence is not necessary in arbitration does not mean that the parties are foreclosed from referring to them. If questionable evidence is admitted, an explanation of the legal rules of evidence may assist the arbitrator in deciding how much weight it should be given. For example, pointing up the likelihood of errors in hearsay evidence will warn the arbitrator not to rely upon it. The careful advocate will warn the arbitrator about the unreliability of certain evidence.

The arbitrator has a duty not to allow testimony to stray too far afield or to be influenced by prejudicial or unreliable testimony. The rules of evidence, flexibly applied, can assist the arbitrator in meeting this obligation. The general rule is to hear everything that will help clarify the issues and to reach a resolution of the dispute. Even if arbitrators admit evidence or testimony over the objection of a party, they may be skeptical as to its probative value. In weighing evidence, an arbitrator should be aware of the following.

**1. Direct Evidence** — Evidence that directly proves a fact, without an inference or presumption. If true, such evidence establishes that fact. Direct evidence from one witness may be sufficient for proof of any fact.

**2. Circumstantial Evidence** — Evidence that tends to establish the "principal fact" by proving other facts from which the principal fact can be inferred. The inference is founded on experience and observed facts, establishing a connection between the proved facts and the fact to be proved.

**3. Relevant and Material Evidence** — Evidence is relevant if it tends to reasonably prove or disprove the fact at issue. Material evidence will influence the decision of the case.

**4. Best Evidence** — Primary evidence as distinguished from secondary; the original as distinguished from copies.

**5. Hearsay Evidence** – Hearsay is second-hand. It is testimony of a statement made by someone other than the witness, repeated at the hearing to show the truth of the matters contained in it. The reliability of a statement rests upon the believability of the person who made the statement. Courts tend to exclude hearsay evidence because of the risk of inaccuracy in the repetition of the story and because there is no opportunity to cross-examine the person making the original statement. There are numerous exceptions to the hearsay rule. Records kept in the ordinary course of business are one such exception. The arbitrator may give hearsay little weight where the opposing party presents contradictory evidence that is subject to cross-examination. An affidavit is a type of hearsay evidence that is explicitly authorized by AAA rules, which caution that the arbitrator shall give an affidavit "only such weight as seems proper after consideration of any objections made to its admission."

**6. Parol Evidence** – Testimony that seeks to explain the meaning of the contract. When a contract is expressed in language that is intended to be the complete and final expression of the rights and duties of the parties, no evidence, oral or written, of prior understandings or negotiations is admissible in court to contradict or vary the terms of the agreement. An arbitrator is somewhat more apt to listen to such evidence.

**7. Opinion Evidence** – Evidence of what the witness thinks about the facts in dispute, as distinguished from personal knowledge of the facts. It is generally not admissible in court except where the witness is an expert in the field. The admissibility of opinion evidence depends on whether the opinion deals with a crucial issue in the case. When a witness is asked an opinion about an important issue and the other party objects, the arbitrator may rule on admissibility. Generally an arbitrator will allow material opinions but will limit the weight given to them according to the qualifications of the witness who expressed them. On the other hand, an arbitrator may bar a witness who is not an expert from giving an opinion on the ultimate question to be decided. Greater latitude is given in arbitration because the arbitrator is likely to be an experienced person, with special knowledge, who will not be unduly influenced by the opinions or conclusions of witnesses.

**8. Inference**—A deduction of fact that may logically and reasonably be drawn from another fact or group of facts found or otherwise established in the matter. An inference is the result of reasoning based upon evidence.

**9. Presumption**—When a group of facts leads to a certain conclusion, the arbitrator may make a presumption.

**10. Cumulative Evidence**—A repetition of evidence that has been testified to previously. Evidence is not cumulative merely because it tends to establish the same ultimate fact. Cumulative evidence is additional evidence of the same kind to prove the same point. In order to conduct an orderly and expeditious hearing, an arbitrator may limit evidence that is repetitive and cumulative in nature and encourage the advocate to move forward with the case.

**11. Burden of Proof**—A party proves a case by providing sufficient evidence to convince the arbitrator on the relevant issues. Each party is expected to prove its case, and if the totality of evidence does not support the grievance submitted to arbitration, the arbitrator will deny it.

**12. Leading Question**—A question worded so that it suggests to the witness the desired answer, often when the answer is merely a yes or no. The danger of leading questions is that the questioner, not the witness, is testifying. Leading questions may save time in preliminary matters that are not in dispute, or when asked during cross-examination. Leading questions asked of a witness about a basic matter, however, are improper and may be stopped by the arbitrator.

**13. Objections**—In arbitration, a party makes objections in order to exclude a particular question, modify the form or manner of questioning, change momentum, or calm a witness who is testifying on cross-examination. An objection can also warn the arbitrator about the weakness of the proffered material.

## THE POWER OF THE ARBITRATOR

An arbitrator is given awesome powers by the parties and by the law. Some are procedural, such as the rights to issue subpoenas, fix the date of hearing, grant postponements (either at the request of a party or on the arbitrator's own initiative), or proceed with the hearing in the absence of a party who fails to appear after being notified. *Ex parte* awards can be enforced as long as the agreement to arbitrate demonstrates the intent to allow such awards. If a contract specifies the AAA rules, hearings can be held in the absence of a party. The award will nonetheless be valid and enforceable (see rule 27).

Because the authority to hear and decide any particular grievance exists only through the agreement of the parties, the arbitrator is endowed with only such authority as the parties confer. The duties of the arbitrator are also defined by law. They include attending all of the hearings, listening to all pertinent and material evidence, and disclosing any prior or existing relationship with the parties. The arbitrator should be impartial in fact and in appearance. An arbitrator must avoid inappropriate contact with parties. The Code of Professional Responsibility for Arbitrators of Labor–Management Disputes appears in the appendix.

At the hearing, the arbitrator should be fair to both parties. Because the adversaries should argue energetically for what they believe to be their rights, a vigorous tone or a strong objection to the arbitrator's acceptance of some evidence that may be damaging should be expected. They are essential elements in the adversarial process.

As a rule, arbitrators have no difficulty in maintaining order. An occasional emotional outburst or attempt to interrupt a witness during direct examination can be handled by the arbitrator with a reminder that the witness can be cross-examined later, or that across-the-table bickering between the advocates serves no useful purpose. Experienced arbitrators know that sometimes it is essential for the parties to "blow off steam"; the disputants are then likely to settle down and proceed in an orderly fashion.

It is very important that arbitrators give no indication of how they will decide. They should not comment on the evidence or reveal their feelings about the merits of the case. They should also avoid excessive cordiality with either of the parties while hearings are in progress.

Evidence must be taken in the presence of both parties. They and their representatives have the right to be present at all times. Arbitrators may, however, require a witness to leave the hearing room during the testimony of other witnesses. The arbitrator has broad powers to determine matters of fact and law as well as procedure. This authority must be exercised by the arbitrator alone, however; it may not be delegated to others. The arbitrator should not seek clarification of a point of law by consulting an outside attorney.

## THE ARBITRATION HEARING

The date of the hearing is fixed by the arbitrator. Usually, the AAA tribunal administrator first consults the parties and arranges a date with the arbitrator. The administrator then notifies the parties.

The customary order of proceedings at the hearing is as follows:

1. opening statement by the initiating party, followed by a similar statement by the other side;

2. presentation of witnesses by the initiating party, with cross-examination by the responding party;

3. presentation of witnesses by the responding party, with cross-examination by the initiating party;

4. summation of both parties, usually following the same order as the opening statements.

This is the normal order. The order can be varied either on the arbitrator's own initiative or at the request of a party. In discipline or discharge cases, for example, it is logical for the employer to go first. The order in which the facts are presented does not imply that the "burden of proof" is greater on one side than on the other. Both parties must try to convince the arbitrator of the correctness of their positions.

## HOW TO PRESENT A CASE IN ARBITRATION

**1. The Opening Statement** — The opening statement should be prepared with care. It lays the groundwork for the testimony of witnesses and helps the arbitrator to understand the relevance of oral and written evidence. The statement should identify the issues, indicate what is to be proved, and specify the relief sought. It is advisable to refer the arbitrator to relevant contract provisions and give ample time to read the language.

The request for relief should be specific. If back pay is demanded, for instance, the complaining party should have the exact amount computed. The arbitrator's authority to grant the requested relief under the contract should be defined.

Because of the importance of the opening statement, some advocates present it to the arbitrator in writing, with a copy for the other side. They believe that it is advantageous to make the initial statement a part of the permanent record. This is a matter of personal style. In any case, an opening statement should be made orally, even when it is supplemented by a written statement. An oral presentation adds emphasis to the argument.

Parties sometimes stipulate facts about the circumstances which gave rise to the grievance. This is a good idea. By giving the arbitrator uncontested facts at the outset of the hearing, the parties can save time and reduce cost.

**2. Presenting Documents** – Documentary evidence may be an essential part of the case. The collective bargaining agreement, or the sections that have bearing on the grievance, should always be submitted. Documentary evidence might also include official minutes of contract negotiation meetings, personnel records, medical reports, wage data, and relevant correspondence. Every piece of documentary evidence should be identified, with its authenticity established. This material should be physically presented to the arbitrator (with a copy for the other side). The significance of each document should be explained. In some instances, key words, phrases, and sections of written documents should be highlighted to focus the arbitrator's attention on essential features. Properly presented, documentary evidence can be most persuasive.

**3. Examining Witnesses** – The facts at issue are generally presented through direct examination. After being identified and qualified, a witness should be permitted to tell the story largely without interruption. Leading questions are usually permitted in arbitration, but testimony is often more effective when given in a witness' own way. Questions sometimes can be useful in emphasizing points already made or in leading a witness back to the main line of testimony.

**4. Cross-Examining Witnesses** – Every witness is subject to cross-examination. Among the purposes of such cross-examination are disclosing facts the witnesses may not have related in direct testimony, correcting misstatements, placing facts in perspective, reconciling apparent contradictions, and attacking the reliability and credibility of adverse witnesses. In planning cross-examination, the objective should be kept in mind. In most cases, proof can best be presented by friendly witnesses: you may sometimes want to waive cross-examination if it would only serve to reinforce the testimony of a hostile witness.

**5. Maintaining the Right Tone**—The atmosphere at the hearing often reflects the relationship between the parties. While the chief purpose of the arbitration hearing is the determination of the particular grievance, a collateral purpose can sometimes be achieved; skillful and friendly conduct by the advocates can sometimes create a better relationship between the parties. To this end, the parties should conduct themselves in a dignified manner. The arbitration hearing should be informal but orderly.

An arbitration is no place for emotional outbursts, long and irrelevant speeches, caustic remarks, or personal invective. Apart from their adverse effect on the relationship between the parties, such tactics are not likely to persuade an arbitrator. Overly legalistic approaches are also counterproductive. Arbitrators are usually seasoned professionals. They are not going to be swayed by bombast or courthouse jargon.

A party has every right to object to irrelevant evidence: the arbitrator should not be burdened with material that has no bearing on the issues. Objections made without firm basis may, however, give the arbitrator the impression that you are afraid to let the other side be heard.

**6. The Summary**—Before the arbitrator closes the hearing, both sides are given an opportunity to make a closing statement. Its purpose is to summarize the facts and the issues and to justify the decision the party wants the arbitrator to make.

Arguments may have been injected into the earlier testimony. But arbitrators often require parties to concentrate on presenting evidence, withholding their arguments until the summary. The closing statement then becomes vital. It may be the last chance to convince the arbitrator. Points made by the other side can be refuted at this time.

**7. Posthearing Procedure**—After both sides have had equal opportunity to present their evidence and arguments, the arbitrator will declare the hearing closed. Under AAA rules, the arbitrator has 30 days within which to render the award, unless the collective bargaining agreement indicates otherwise. If parties need to file posthearing briefs or additional documents, the arbitrator can set appropriate time limits; hearings remain open until documents are due. Posthearing material is exchanged through the AAA tribunal administrator. The parties should not communicate with the arbitrator directly unless both sides are present. The AAA will see that the briefs are transmitted to the arbitrator.

**8. How to Reopen Hearings**—When parties jointly agree to add data after a hearing is closed, they may arrange to do so by written stipulations filed with the AAA. The arbitrator will then study the new material.

In the event that new evidence is discovered, or if a situation arises that seems to require explanation, parties should not attempt to communicate directly with the arbitrator. Through the AAA, they should request an additional hearing or otherwise arrange for presentation of necessary evidence. Arbitrators may also reopen hearings on their own initiative.

Contact between the parties and the arbitrator is channeled through the AAA to eliminate any suspicion that one side may have offered arguments which the other had no opportunity to rebut. In some situations, the relationship between the parties will be such that direct contact with the arbitrator is customary and appropriate, but this is not encouraged.

## TEN WAYS TO LOSE CREDIBILITY IN ARBITRATION

1. Using arbitration of grievances that cannot be won as a harassment technique.

2. Overemphasizing the grievance by the union or exaggerating an employee's fault by management.

3. Preparing insufficiently; relying on a minimum of facts and a maximum of arguments.

4. Introducing witnesses who are improperly prepared as to demeanor or the relevance of their testimony in the case.

5. Attempting to conceal essential facts or distort the truth.

6. Refusing to show books, records, and other documents until required to do so by subpoena.

7. Obstructing the procedure with legal technicalities.

8. Withholding full cooperation from the arbitrator.

9. Disregarding common courtesy and decorum.

10. Engaging in debate with the other side. The time to try to convince the other party is during grievance discussions before arbitration. The arbitration hearing should concentrate on convincing the arbitrator.

## THE AWARD

The award is the decision of the arbitrator on the matters submitted under the arbitration agreement. Its purpose is to dispose of the controversy finally and conclusively.

The award should be limited to the issues defined in the demand for arbitration. It should decide each claim submitted and should be definite and final. The award is generally accompanied by an opinion which reviews the evidence and sets forth the arbitrator's reasoning.

The power of the arbitrator ends with the rendering of an award. An award may not be changed by the arbitrator once it is made unless the parties mutually agree to reopen the case and to restore power to the arbitrator. In legal terms, the arbitrator is *functus officio* after the award is signed.

When the parties do agree to ask the arbitrator to reopen a case in order to obtain a clarification or interpretation of an ambiguous award, the agreement to reopen should be in writing and should precisely set forth the question submitted. When such an agreement is filed with the AAA, the tribunal administrator will make arrangements with the arbitrator.

Under the law, an arbitrator cannot be forced to testify in any legal proceeding as to the award. It is unprofessional for lawyers to attempt to harass an arbitrator by seeking to compel such testimony.

## AWARDS BY TRIPARTITE BOARDS

The use of tripartite boards of arbitrators sometimes creates special problems. Usually, an award must be supported by a majority of the arbitrators. The difficulty is that party-appointed arbitrators often regard themselves as advocates. A compromise award by the neutral arbitrator could be rejected by both party-appointed arbitrators. Scheduling problems, considerations of cost, and the ambiguities of the party-appointed arbitrator's role have convinced most parties to avoid the tripartite board system.

In very important cases or in interest arbitration, the parties may want to have the benefit of a group judgment, in which case they might prefer to agree on a panel of three neutral arbitrators.

# CHAPTER 4

# ARBITRATION IN THE PUBLIC SECTOR

## GRIEVANCE ARBITRATION

The major use of arbitration in public-sector labor relations is to settle employee grievances. Arbitration has been proven to be a sound system for dealing with disagreements over the day-to-day administration of collective bargaining contracts between unions and public employers. The AAA publishes two monthly reports describing such cases—*Labor Arbitration in Government* and *Arbitration in the Schools*. They show how the system works.

Under private-sector contractual grievance procedures, the parties have an early opportunity to resolve the problem internally. Even arbitration is carried out under full control of the parties. In contrast, civil-service review procedures involve a legalistic format within which the parties' control is easily detached.

In some states, grievance arbitration has completely replaced the disciplinary review function of civil service for organized workers. Both unions and local governments tend to prefer arbitration to the statutory review procedures.

Even the most comprehensive labor contract cannot

anticipate every problem that may arise — e.g., disciplinary problems, changes in operation, and new demands by the public. A grievance procedure provides the parties with a format for resolving such questions. The union can play a useful role in such situations. The grievance procedure can help to build operating efficiency.

With the development of sound labor relations, arbitration need seldom be used. The key to a successful grievance procedure is the first-line supervisor. In public employment, it may be difficult to persuade supervisors to become totally committed to management's position. Supervisors are themselves often unionized. Having been promoted from the workforce, they may not be conditioned to think of themselves as management. It is vital, however, that supervisors represent the employer's interests. They need to be given training to ensure that they recognize their managerial responsibilities.

Most labor grievances can be resolved between the worker and the supervisor at the first step of the procedure. If the agency's supervisors cannot provide that capability, the chances of a healthy employee relationship are slim indeed.

In jurisdictions that allow collective bargaining, grievance arbitration will continue to be used to resolve disputes. Under the pressure of budget reductions, managers will try to reduce operating costs. Grievances will surely result. Most can be settled, but the rest will be decided by arbitrators.

## COLLECTIVE BARGAINING

Bargaining in state and local government is more political than in the private sector, where it is primarily economic. A political process is particularly sensitive to public opinion.

Legislators know that the public does not like strikes in the public service, whether by teachers, police, or fire-fighters. With the growing acceptance of public-sector bargaining, there has been a greater use of compulsory interest arbitration, particularly for public-safety employees. Many observers believe that compulsory arbitration of interest disputes inhibits collective bargaining.

Workers and taxpayers participate in collective bargaining through the elected leadership of their representatives at the table. Not so in interest arbitration or factfinding. There, lawyers hold the spotlight. The testimony involves complicated arguments and data. Attention is deflected from the elected leaders, who play a more passive role.

## ENCOURAGE NEGOTIATIONS

Where compulsory arbitration must be used for political reasons, a procedure should be developed to ensure that parties first negotiate, at least until they have exhausted their ability to do so. Parties often come to arbitration too soon. Multiple, unresolved issues can be a clear indication that collective bargaining has not yet had an opportunity to do its job.

Public employment relations boards have been created by many states to regulate collective bargaining in the public sector. They have a difficult task. They must exert pressure on both parties, making sure that negotiators understand their role in collective bargaining and that they carry out their leadership responsibilities to their respective constituencies. One of those duties is to help both parties prepare for the bargaining table.

A party's attitude toward strikes is one index of the maturity of the relationship. Strikes by public employees have not been catastrophic. Strikes by teachers, sanitation workers, and even police have been endured. Certainly there can be substantial hardship and risk. But the social cost of such strikes could be less severe than the cost of eliminating the right to bargain collectively. If occasional strikes can be accepted as the price that we must pay for collective bargaining, society will not unravel.

Strikes are based on economic inequities. The employees are not enemy agents; they are citizens, taxpayers, consumers, and public servants, as well as union members. Many public employers are learning to live with strikes. Some have learned to win them.

State legislatures continue to experiment with third-party settlement procedures, especially for "essential services" such as police and firefighters. A successful system of interest arbitration should facilitate bargaining between the bureaucratic hierarchies of the parties by providing a device for resolving impasses in a way that will create accountability and gain general acceptance for the result.

Many states authorize interest arbitration for certain public-sector impasses. In those states, local public employers are learning to negotiate under new groundrules. The legislature has concluded that a mandatory collective bargaining structure is in the public interest, providing a statutory alternative to strikes.

In other states, such legislation is absent. It may be necessary for local governments to create different arrangements for bargaining. It is possible to contract for dispute settlement systems. The American Arbitration Association is one resource. It has administered contested representation elections, supplied factfinders and arbitrators, and has provided complete public employment board services.

The trend toward the use of binding arbitration to settle bargaining impasses involving essential public services will probably continue. There are, however, some inherent difficulties. Arbitration is not a panacea. If arbitrators are given unlimited authority to decide bargaining issues, arbitration will have a chilling effect upon negotiations. Parties could adopt unrealistic positions at the table, anticipating that the dispute will be presented to an arbitrator.

Interest arbitration might encourage the bargaining representatives of the parties to defer to legal counsel, increasing the likelihood of litigation. This could be counterproductive. Collective bargaining involves the direct participation of the parties. Union leaders are expected to fight for their members; elected representatives are expected to stand up for the taxpayer. Bargaining provides a forum within which the leaders of both sides can perform. In arbitration, elected officials are less visible. The spotlight shifts from the organization's leaders to its lawyers. The taxpayer may feel disenfranchised. The union member may become alienated from the process. The process can become submerged beneath legal verbiage and court procedures.

Traditional arbitration places authority in the hands of outsiders, persons with no stake in the local community. Arbitrators do not have a local constituency. They have no prior notion of the parties' unique problems and they do not have to live with the agreement. Qualms about the legitimacy of interest arbitration have troubled some courts.

State legislatures have a practical problem: how best to resolve bargaining impasses in public employment. The public has never been enthusiastic about strikes, but has been willing to accept the inconvenience of occasional private-sector work stoppages as the price that must be paid for collective bargaining. Public-sector strikes are, however, another matter. People do not like to see garbage in the streets, pickets around their schools, or empty firehouses. Public-sector strikes can create hardship, inconvenience, and threats to health and safety. Such strikes often generate immediate and compelling pressures upon public officials.

The public's willingness to suffer through a public-service strike will vary, depending upon the service, the season, and the political situation. Work stoppages of so-called essential services are seldom tolerated. This presents the lawmakers with a problem. If the strike is to be outlawed, workers will have to be given a right to bargain. A new system must be developed to settle the impasse and create an incentive for the parties to engage in good-faith negotiations. An appropriate system of interest arbitration should maximize party involvement, enforce accountability to the constituencies, maintain public acceptance, and, beyond all else, eliminate strikes.

## LAST-OFFER ARBITRATION

In recent years, there has been increasing support for a process called "last-offer" arbitration. Under that system, an arbitrator is authorized to choose between the last offers presented by each of the parties. This can be done either on a package basis or item by item. Such a system encourages compromise. Neither the union nor the employer can afford to have the arbitrator select the last offer of its adversary. They therefore reduce their final demands, narrowing the gap between their respective positions. Last-offer arbitration seems to result in more settlements.

Another benefit of last-offer arbitration is that the authority of the arbitrator is restricted to making a choice. The arbitrator is not permitted to exercise broad discretion. This reassures parties that hesitate to delegate legislative authority to an outsider.

## CRITERIA FOR AN INTEREST ARBITRATION STATUTE

Interest arbitration in the public sector is not based on voluntary agreement; it is imposed on certain parties. It is the result of legislative action representing a political judgment as to how collective bargaining impasses should be resolved for certain categories of public employees where strikes or termination of services are inappropriate.

Interest arbitration must be appraised in the context of the setting in which it is used:

Which kinds of employee are covered?

What administrative or regulatory procedures are applicable to the bargaining?

Which issues are bargainable?

What timetables must be followed?

How does the bargaining relate to the public employer's budgetary process?

Is mediation available or required?

Are the parties required to participate in factfinding?

What is the authority of the arbitrator: open ended or last offer? Is the last offer on a package basis or issue by issue?

How are arbitrators selected?

What are their qualifications?

What criteria must be considered by the arbitrators?

Is the award advisory or binding?

If binding, what is the scope of review?

Is the award reviewable by the courts, by the legislature, or by referendum?

What are the criteria for review?

What are the penalties for a strike?

These are a few of the questions that must be asked about any particular interest arbitration scheme. The overall question, of course, is whether that bargaining structure for those parties at that point in their history provides a process appropriate to the legislative goals.

Factfinding and advisory arbitration are attractive concepts, but too frequently they are inconclusive in practice. Open-ended, compulsory arbitration encourages parties to come to the tribunal with all of their options free and discourages hard bargaining. Only last-offer arbitration encourages the negotiators to make concessions. Many communities are experimenting with compulsory last-offer arbitration systems.

## VOLUNTARY ARBITRATION

Voluntary interest arbitration also may have a role in collective bargaining. It may be appropriate where the analytical powers of an informed neutral can rationalize away an aberration in the bargaining climate. It can be used to rescue parties who have maneuvered themselves into a corner. It can dispose of complicated issues that remain unresolved in the final rush of settlement. Voluntary interest arbitration can be a useful trick in the negotiator's bag. Where the neutral is particularly expert, the parties may agree to experiment with med–arb, a voluntary process wherein the impartial has a dual role, acting primarily as a mediator but reserving the authority of an arbitrator. In these situations, the impartial must be creative and solution minded.

## COMPULSORY ARBITRATION

Compulsory arbitration of impasses in the public sector is no panacea. Such systems may tend to reduce the motivation of public and union officials to establish wages and working conditions on the basis of collective bargaining power. Collective bargaining is a marketing process in which the parties participate. Interest arbitration tends to be a lifeless mirror of the status quo; the parties themselves could be more open to change than a cautious neutral.

Compulsory arbitration cannot produce a strikeless society. Bargaining is not a judicial process that measures the equities of an employment contract. If that were its purpose, it could be replaced by any number of more rational systems.

Collective bargaining is a crude but powerful engine. It permits the union to test its desires and needs against the priorities of the employer. Both parties benefit from an agreement. Often, only disagreements within the bargaining unit or within the management group stand in the way.

The reasons why collective bargaining in the public sector fails include conflicting management or fiscal priorities, unionization of supervisors, disputes over the scope of bargaining, ambiguities in applicable law, and inappropriate labor regulations. The parties themselves must collaborate to formulate a public employment package that can successfully compete in the legislative–political arena with other claimants for public resources.

## ARBITRATION IN THE FEDERAL SERVICE

Collective bargaining in the federal service has never been the all-encompassing vehicle for change that it has been in the private sector, or even in local government. Federal contractual grievance systems have consequently played a secondary role.

Traditionally, Congress has determined wages and working conditions in federal employment. The primary function of federal unions is to lobby for their members. The Pendleton Act, in 1883, created the civil-service system, setting basic rules for hiring, dismissal, and promotion under the merit system.

With the Kennedy Executive Order of 1962, a restricted form of collective bargaining came into play. The scope of bargaining was narrow. Subsequent executive orders extended the scope of bargaining, and the Pay Comparability Act shifted the authority for fixing wages from Congress to the President. But collective bargaining in the federal sector is still limited. Local union leaders and agency labor relations personnel do not as yet play a major role in federal labor relations.

The federal employee still looks to the Administration and to Congress for improvements in salary and working conditions. For those federal employees now covered by collective bargaining contracts, the grievance process gives unions some opportunity to serve their members.

Federal employees do not have the legal right to strike. Arbitration was not a *quid pro quo* for giving up the right to strike.

In the federal sector, the contractual grievance procedure operates subject to rules and regulations governing arbitrability. There are established procedures for selecting among appropriate remedies. The federal sector is a cat's cradle of alternative procedures.

In spite of all that, federal sector grievance arbitration has been growing. For those federal employees who are covered by collective bargaining contracts, binding arbitration has become a normal way to resolve certain categories of disputes between employees and agency management.

The use of binding arbitration continues to grow. The annual caseload in the federal sector has been increasing. Advisory arbitration has been replaced by binding arbitration.

In the private sector, traditional wisdom is that arbitrators' decisions should be final, binding, and enforceable. In the federal sector, there are higher rates of review and of overturned awards and the grounds for appeal are more extensive.

# APPENDIX

## Voluntary Labor Arbitration Rules (Including Streamlined Labor Arbitration Rules)

*As Amended and in Effect January 1, 1988*

**1. Agreement of Parties**—The parties shall be deemed to have made these rules a part of their arbitration agreement whenever, in a collective bargaining agreement or submission, they have provided for arbitration by the American Arbitration Association (hereinafter the AAA) or under its rules. These rules and any amendment thereof shall apply in the form obtaining at the time the arbitration is initiated.

**2. Name of Tribunal**—Any tribunal constituted by the parties under these rules shall be called the Voluntary Labor Arbitration Tribunal.

**3. Administrator**—When parties agree to arbitrate under these rules and an arbitration is instituted thereunder, they thereby authorize the AAA to administer the arbitration. The authority and obligations of the administrator are as provided in the agreement of the parties and in these rules.

**4. Delegation of Duties**—The duties of the AAA may be carried out through such representatives or committees as the AAA may direct.

**5. Panel of Labor Arbitrators**—The AAA shall establish and maintain a Panel of Labor Arbitrators and shall appoint arbitrators therefrom, as hereinafter provided.

**6. Office of Tribunal**—The general office of the Voluntary Labor Arbitration Tribunal is the headquarters of the AAA, which may, however, assign the administration of an arbitration to any of its regional offices.

**7. Initiation under an Arbitration Clause in a Collective Bargaining Agreement**—Arbitration under an arbitration clause in a collective bargaining agreement under these rules may be initiated by either party in the following manner:

(a) By giving written notice to the other party of intention to arbitrate (Demand), which notice shall contain a statement setting forth the nature of the dispute and the remedy sought, and

(b) By filing at any regional office of the AAA three copies of said notice, together with a copy of the collective bargaining agreement, or such parts thereof as relate to the dispute, including the arbitration provisions. After the arbitrator is appointed, no new or different claim may be submitted except with the consent of the arbitrator and all other parties.

**8. Answer**—The party upon whom the Demand for arbitration is made may file an answering statement with the AAA within seven days after notice from the AAA, simultaneously sending a copy to the other party. If no answer is filed within the stated time, it will be assumed that the claim is denied. Failure to file an answer shall not operate to delay the arbitration.

**9. Initiation under a Submission**—Parties to any collective bargaining agreement may initiate an arbitration under these rules by filing at any regional office of the AAA two copies of a written agreement to arbitrate under these rules (Submission), signed by the parties and setting forth the nature of the dispute and the remedy sought.

**10. Fixing of Locale**—The parties may mutually agree upon the locale where the arbitration is to be held. If the locale is not designated in the collective bargaining agreement or Submission and, if there is a dispute as to the appropriate locale, the AAA shall have the power to determine the locale and its decision shall be binding.

**11. Qualifications of Arbitrator**—No person shall serve as a neutral arbitrator in any arbitration in which he or she has any financial personal interest in the result of the arbitration, unless the parties, in writing, waive such disqualification.

**12. Appointment from Panel**—If the parties have not appointed an arbitrator and have not provided any other method of appointment, the arbitrator shall be appointed in the following manner: Immediately after the filing of the Demand or Submission, the AAA shall submit simultaneously to each party an identical list of names of persons chosen from the Panel of Labor Arbitrators. Each party shall have seven days from the mailing date in which to cross off any names to which it objects, number the remaining names to indicate the order of preference, and return the list to the AAA. If a party does not return the list within the time specified, all persons named therein shall be deemed acceptable. From among the persons who have been approved on both lists, and in accordance with the designated order of mutual preference, the AAA shall invite the acceptance of an arbitrator to serve. If the parties fail to agree upon any of the persons named, if those named decline or are unable to act, or if for any other reason the appointment cannot be made from the submitted lists, the administrator shall have the power to make the appointment from among other members of the panel without the submission of any additional list.

**13. Direct Appointment by Parties**—If the agreement of the parties names an arbitrator or specifies a method of appointing an arbitrator, that designation or method shall be followed. The notice of appointment, with the name and address of such arbitrator, shall be filed with the AAA by the appointing party.

If the agreement specifies a period of time within which an arbitrator shall be appointed and any party fails to make such appointment within that period, the AAA may make the appointment.

If no period of time is specified in the agreement, the AAA shall notify the parties to make the appointment and if within seven days thereafter such arbitrator has not been so appointed, the AAA shall make the appointment.

**14. Appointment of Neutral Arbitrator by Party-Appointed Arbitrators**—If the parties have appointed their arbitrators, or if either or both of them have been appointed as provided in Section 13, and have authorized such arbitrators to appoint a neutral arbitrator within a specified time and no appointment is made within such time or any agreed extension thereof, the AAA may appoint a neutral arbitrator who shall act as chairperson.

If no period of time is specified for appointment of the neutral arbitrator and the parties do not make the appointment within seven days from the date of the appointment of the last party-appointed arbitrator, the AAA shall appoint such neutral arbitrator, who shall act as chairperson.

If the parties have agreed that the arbitrators shall appoint the neutral arbitrator from the panel, the AAA shall furnish to the party-appointed arbitrators, in the manner prescribed in Section 12, a list selected from the panel, and the appointment of the neutral arbitrator shall be made as prescribed in that section.

**15. Number of Arbitrators**—If the arbitration agreement does not specify the number of arbitrators, the dispute shall be heard and determined by one arbitrator, unless the parties otherwise agree.

**16. Notice to Arbitrator of Appointment**—Notice of the appointment of the neutral arbitrator shall be mailed to the arbitrator by the AAA and the signed acceptance of the arbitrator shall be filed with the AAA prior to the opening of the first hearing.

**17. Disclosure by Arbitrator of Disqualification**—Prior to accepting the appointment, the prospective neutral arbitrator shall disclose any circumstance likely to create a presumption of bias or that the arbitrator believes might disqualify him or her as an impartial arbitrator. Upon receipt of such information, the AAA shall immediately disclose it to the parties. If either party declines to waive the presumptive disqualification, the vacancy thus created shall be filled in accordance with the applicable provisions of these rules.

**18. Vacancies**—If any arbitrator should resign, die, withdraw, refuse, be unable, or be disqualified to perform the duties of office, the AAA shall, on proof satisfactory to it, declare the office vacant. Vacancies shall be filled in the same manner as that governing the making of the original appointment, and the matter shall be reheard by the new arbitrator.

**19. Time and Place of Hearing**—The arbitrator shall fix the time and place for each hearing. At least five days prior thereto, the AAA shall mail notice of the time and place of hearing to each party, unless the parties otherwise agree.

**20. Representation by Counsel**—Any party may be represented at the hearing by counsel or by another authorized representative.

**21. Stenographic Record**—Any party wishing a stenographic record shall make arrangements directly with a stenographer and shall notify the other parties of such arrangements in advance of the hearing. The requesting party or parties shall pay the cost of such record. If such transcript is agreed by the parties to be, or in appropriate cases determined by the arbitrator to be, the official record of the proceeding, it must be made available to the arbitrator and to the other party for inspection, at a time and place determined by the arbitrator.

**22. Attendance at Hearings**—Persons having a direct interest in the arbitration are entitled to attend hearings. The arbitrator shall have the power to require the retirement of any witness or witnesses during the testimony of other witnesses. It shall be discretionary with the arbitrator to determine the propriety of the attendance of any other person.

**23. Adjournments**—The arbitrator for good cause shown may adjourn the hearing upon the request of a party or upon his or her own initiative, and shall adjourn when all of the parties agree thereto.

**24. Oaths**—Before proceeding with the first hearing, each arbitrator may take an oath of office and, if required by law, shall do so. The arbitrator may require witnesses to testify under oath administered by any duly qualified person and, if required by law or requested by either party, shall do so.

**25. Majority Decision**—Whenever there is more than one arbitrator, all decisions of the arbitrators shall be by majority vote. The award shall also be made by majority vote unless the concurrence of all is expressly required.

**26. Order of Proceedings**—A hearing shall be opened by the filing of the oath of the arbitrator, where required; by the recording of the place, time, and date of the hearing and the presence of the arbitrator, the parties, and counsel, if any; and by the receipt by the arbitrator of the Demand and answer, if any, or the Submission.

Exhibits may, when offered by either party, be received in evidence by the arbitrator. The names and addresses of all witnesses and exhibits in order received shall be made a part of the record.

The arbitrator may vary the normal procedure under which the initiating party first presents its claim, but in any case shall afford full and equal opportunity to all parties for the presentation of relevant proofs.

**27. Arbitration in the Absence of a Party**—Unless the law provides to the contrary, the arbitration may proceed in the absence of any party who, after due notice, fails to be present or fails to obtain an adjournment. An award shall not be made solely on the default of a party. The arbitrator shall require the other party to submit such evidence as may be required for the making of an award.

**28. Evidence**—The parties may offer such evidence as they desire and shall produce such additional evidence as the arbitrator may deem necessary to an understanding and determination of the dispute. An arbitrator authorized by law to subpoena witnesses and documents may do so independently or upon the request of any party. The arbitrator shall be the judge of the relevance and materiality of the evidence offered and conformity to legal rules of evidence shall not be necessary. All evidence shall be taken in the presence of all of the arbitrators and all of the parties except where any of the parties is absent in default or has waived the right to be present.

**29. Evidence by Affidavit and Filing of Documents**—The arbitrator may receive and consider the evidence of witnesses by affidavit, giving it only such weight as seems proper after consideration of any objection made to its admission.

All documents that are not filed with the arbitrator at the hearing, but arranged at the hearing or subsequently by agreement of the parties to be submitted, shall be filed with the AAA for transmission to the arbitrator. All parties shall be afforded opportunity to examine such documents.

**30. Inspection**—Whenever the arbitrator deems it necessary, he or she may make an inspection in connection with the subject matter of the dispute after written notice to the parties, who may, if they so desire, be present at such inspection.

**31. Closing of Hearings**—The arbitrator shall inquire of all parties whether they have any further proofs to offer or witnesses to be heard. Upon receiving negative replies, the arbitrator shall declare the hearings closed and a minute thereof shall be recorded. If briefs or other documents are to be filed, the hearings shall be declared closed as of the final date set by the arbitrator for filing with the AAA. The time limit within which the arbitrator is required to make an award shall commence to run, in the absence of another agreement by the parties, upon the closing of the hearings.

**32. Reopening of Hearings**—The hearings may for good cause shown be reopened by the arbitrator at will or on the motion of either party at any time before the award is made, but, if the reopening of the hearings would prevent the making of the award within the specific time agreed upon by the parties in the contract out of which the controversy has arisen, the matter may not be reopened unless both parties agree upon the extension of such time. When no specific date is fixed in the contract, the arbitrator may reopen the hearings and shall have thirty days from the closing of the reopened hearings within which to make an award.

**33. Waiver of Oral Hearings**—The parties may provide, by written agreement, for the waiver of oral hearings. If the parties are unable to agree as to the procedure, the AAA shall specify a fair and equitable procedure.

**34. Waiver of Rules**—Any party who proceeds with the arbitration after knowledge that any provision or requirement of these rules has not been complied with and who fails to state an objection thereto in writing shall be deemed to have waived the right to object.

**35. Extensions of Time**—The parties may modify any period of time by mutual agreement. The AAA may for good cause extend any period of time established by these rules, except the time for making the award. The AAA shall notify the parties of any such extension of time and its reason therefor.

**36. Serving of Notice**—Each party to a Submission or other agreement that provides for arbitration under these rules shall be deemed to have consented and shall consent that any papers, notices, or process necessary or proper for the initiation or continuation of an arbitration under these rules; for any court action in connection therewith; or for the entry of judgment on an award made thereunder may be served upon such party by mail addressed to such party or its attorney at the last known address or by personal service, within or without the state wherein the arbitration is to be held.

**37. Time of Award**—The award shall be rendered promptly by the arbitrator and, unless otherwise agreed by the parties or specified by law, no later than thirty days from the date of closing the hearings or, if oral hearings have been waived, from the date of transmitting the final statements and proofs to the arbitrator.

**38. Form of Award**—The award shall be in writing and shall be signed either by the neutral arbitrator or by a concurring majority if there be more than one arbitrator. The parties shall advise the AAA whenever they do not require the arbitrator to accompany the award with an opinion.

**39. Award upon Settlement**—If the parties settle their dispute during the course of the arbitration, the arbitrator may, upon their request, set forth the terms of the agreed settlement in an award.

**40. Delivery of Award to Parties**—Parties shall accept as legal delivery of the award the placing of the award or a true copy thereof in the mail by the AAA, addressed to such party at its last known address or to its attorney; personal service of the award; or the filing of the award in any other manner that may be prescribed by law.

**41. Release of Documents for Judicial Proceedings**—The AAA shall, upon the written request of a party, furnish to such party, at its expense, certified facsimiles of any papers in the AAA's possession that may be required in judicial proceedings relating to the arbitration.

**42. Judicial Proceedings and Exclusion of Liability**—(a) Neither the AAA nor any arbitrator in a proceeding under these rules is a necessary party in judicial proceedings relating to the arbitration.

(b) Neither the AAA nor any arbitrator shall be liable to any party for any act or omission in connection with any arbitration conducted under these rules.

**43. Administrative Fees**—As a not-for-profit organization, the AAA shall prescribe an administrative fee schedule to compensate it for the cost of providing administrative services. The schedule in effect at the time of filing shall be applicable.

**44. Expenses**—The expenses of witnesses for either side shall be paid by the party producing such witnesses.

Expenses of the arbitration, other than the cost of the stenographic record, including required traveling and other expenses of the arbitrator and of AAA representatives and the expenses of any witness or the cost of any proof produced at the direct request of the arbitrator, shall be borne equally by the parties, unless they agree otherwise, or unless the arbitrator, in the award, assesses such expenses or any part thereof against any specified party or parties.

**45. Communication with Arbitrator**—There shall be no communication between the parties and a neutral arbitrator other than at oral hearings. Any other oral or written communication from the parties to the arbitrator shall be directed to the AAA for transmittal to the arbitrator.

**46. Interpretation and Application of Rules**—The arbitrator shall interpret and apply these rules insofar as they relate to the arbitrator's powers and duties. When there is more than one arbitrator and a difference arises among them concerning the meaning or application of any such rule, it shall be decided by a majority vote. If that is unobtainable, the arbitrator or either party may refer the question to the AAA for final decision. All other rules shall be interpreted and applied by the AAA.

## Streamlined Labor Arbitration Rules

**Initiation of Arbitration**—Cases may be initiated by joint submission in writing, or in accordance with a collective bargaining agreement.

**Appointment of Arbitrator**—The arbitrator will be appointed by the AAA from members of its Panel of Labor Arbitrators who have agreed to serve under these rules.

**Scheduling of Hearings**—The hearing shall be held within 25 days of appointment of the arbitrator. The arbitrator shall fix the time and place of hearing, notice of which shall be given to the parties by the AAA at least five calendar days in advance.

**No Transcripts and Briefs**—There shall be no briefs or transcripts.

**Award**—The award is due within five business days of the closing of the hearing. The opinion will be brief and generally not exceed two pages in length.

**Arbitrator Compensation**—The arbitrator will be compensated $500 for the case, including the hearing day, expenses, travel charges, study, and preparation. The $500 arbitrator compensation will be shared between the parties unless they agree otherwise. The arbitrator shall be entitled to a fee of $200 if the hearing is postponed by either party on less than 72 hours' notice.

**Judicial Proceedings and Exclusion of Liability**—(a) Neither the AAA nor any arbitrator in a proceeding under these rules is a necessary party in judicial proceedings relating to the arbitration.

(b) Neither the AAA nor any arbitrator shall be liable to any party for any act or omission in connection with any arbitration conducted under these rules.

**Administrative Fees**—The AAA administrative fee is $50 per party.

**Postponement**—A fee of $50 is payable to the AAA by any party causing postponement of any scheduled hearing.

**Interpretation and Application of Rules**—Any questions not covered by these rules shall be decided in accordance with the Voluntary Labor Arbitration Rules of the Americn Arbitration Association.

The arbitrator shall interpret and apply these rules insofar as they relate to the arbitrator's powers and duties. All other rules shall be interpreted and applied by the AAA, as administrator.

# The Jargon of
# Labor Arbitration:
# A Glossary

*Ad Hoc* **Arbitrator**   An arbitrator jointly selected by the parties to serve on one case. Many employers and unions believe that decisions are more likely to be fair and equitable if the arbitrator is chosen on a case-by-case basis. If both parties are satisfied with the arbitrator's ability, they may select that person again for another case. The *ad hoc* system enables the parties to retain their freedom of choice.

**Adjournment of Hearing**   The arbitrator has the power to postpone a hearing at the request of either party (see AAA Voluntary Labor Arbitration Rule 23). If the arbitrator unreasonably refuses to postpone a hearing, a losing party could have grounds for vacating the award.

**Administrative Agency**   An impartial agency that maintains panels of labor arbitrators. Administrative services can be specified by appropriate reference to an agency in the collective bargaining contract. The AAA is the only private agency in the United States. The Federal Mediation and Conciliation Service and various state and local government agencies also issue lists of arbitrators.

**Administrative Appointment**   The designation of the arbitrator by an administrative agency. Sections 12, 13, and 14 of the Voluntary Labor Arbitration Rules provide for administrative appointments in the event of impasse. When parties have failed to agree on a mutual choice from a list submitted to them, the AAA can make the appointment. Under expedited arrangements, the parties can empower the AAA to make the appointment without a preliminary submission of lists.

**Advisory Arbitration**  A system under which an arbitrator is selected to render an award that recommends a solution to the dispute. Advisory arbitration has been used in public employment, sometimes to help resolve bargaining impasses.

**Affidavit**  A statement in writing made under oath before a notary public or other authorized officer. Such statements are sometimes submitted and received as evidence in labor arbitration hearings. Section 29 of the Voluntary Labor Arbitration Rules states that the arbitrator "may receive and consider the evidence of witnesses by affidavit, giving it only such weight as seems proper after consideration of any objections made to its admission." Where the witness is available and could be cross-examined, the arbitrator may refuse to accept such an affidavit.

**Appeal**  A proceeding for obtaining review of a decision. In arbitration, the right to appeal is not available. An award can be challenged in court by a motion to vacate. In labor arbitration, such motions are generally based on allegations that the award exceeded the arbitrator's authority.

**Appointment of Arbitrators**  Arbitrators are chosen by the parties in accordance with the procedures designated in the arbitration clause in their collective bargaining agreement. Most provisions call for the appointment of a single arbitrator. Some agreements, however, provide for the designation of "party-appointed arbitrators," who then select a single, neutral arbitrator to act as chairman. If the party-appointed arbitrators or the parties themselves are unable to agree on an arbitrator, a court can make the appointment on the motion of one of the parties. The parties can avoid the necessity of going to court by designating an administrative agency in their contract.

**Arbitrability** Does the moving party have a right to arbitrate the dispute? Procedural arbitrability often turns on whether specified steps have been carried out prior to the initiation of arbitration. Substantive arbitrability concerns the scope of the arbitration clause. The arbitration agreement should describe the kinds of dispute it covers and what steps must be completed before a party has the right to demand arbitration. Questions of arbitrability may be determined either by an arbitrator or in court, depending on the arbitration provision in the contract and the applicable law. Under Section 301 of the Taft–Hartley Act, arbitration is required under an arbitration clause if the parties cannot be said "with positive assurance" to have excluded the subject from arbitration. *United Steelworkers v. Warrior & Gulf Navigation Co.*, 363 U.S. 574 (1960).

**Arbitration Clause** That part of a collective bargaining contract providing for arbitration as the final step of the grievance procedure. A reference therein to the arbitration rules of the AAA establishes all the procedures necessary for arbitration.

**Arbitrator** A person who is given the power to resolve a dispute between parties. The labor arbitrator is usually selected because the parties have confidence in that person's ability to interpret collective bargaining agreements.

Once selected, the arbitrator enters into a system of contractual self-government that the parties themselves have created. The arbitrator is insulated from legal responsibility. Under AAA administration, the arbitrator acts subject to the provisions of the arbitration rules.

**Arbitrator's Authority**  The power of an arbitrator to hear and determine a dispute is derived from law and from the agreement of the parties. The extent of authority can be determined by examining the arbitration agreement.

In *United Steelworkers v. Enterprise Wheel & Car Corp.,* Justice Douglas defined the authority of the labor arbitrator as follows: "When an arbitrator is commissioned to interpret and apply the collective bargaining agreement, he is to bring his informed judgment to bear in order to reach a fair solution of a problem. . . . Nevertheless, an arbitrator is confined to interpretation and application of the collective bargaining agreement; he does not sit to dispense his own brand of industrial justice. He may of course look for guidance from many sources, yet his award is legitimate only so long as it draws its essence from the collective bargaining agreement. When the arbitrator's words manifest an infidelity to his obligation, courts have no choice but to refuse enforcement of the award" (363 U.S. 595 (1960)).

**Award**  The decision of an arbitrator in a dispute. The arbitrator's award is based on the testimony and arguments of both parties. In labor arbitration, the arbitrator's reasons are generally expressed in the form of a written opinion that accompanies the award. The opinion will analyze the evidence and issues raised by the parties. In a growing number of cases, parties request labor arbitrators to issue a summary award, disposing of the issue while dispensing with much of the dicta. This procedure can greatly reduce the cost of arbitration.

**Award upon Settlement**  An award made at the request of both parties, incorporating terms of a settlement made by parties.

**Back-Pay Award**  Under most arbitration clauses, an arbitrator may order reinstatement of an employee who has been discharged or suspended without just cause. The arbitrator may reduce the penalty by reinstating the grievant, without back pay, or may reduce back pay to the extent of compensation that the employee has been receiving from another job or from unemployment. Some contracts restrict the arbitrator's authority to fashion a remedy.

**Bias**  An arbitrator has a duty to disclose any facts or circumstances that might create a presumption of bias or disqualify him or her from serving as an impartial arbitrator. Under Section 17 of the AAA Voluntary Labor Arbitration Rules, such a disclosure is required. The Code of Professional Responsibility for Arbitrators of Labor–Management Disputes is also applicable.

**Binding Effect of Arbitration Award**  An arbitrator's award is final and binding upon both parties. Labor arbitration awards can be confirmed in court. A judgment entered upon an award in one state can be enforced in other states. In practice, most labor arbitration awards are accepted by the parties; litigation is rare.

**Breach of Contract**  Failure to abide by the legal obligations of a contract. A labor grievance is an alleged breach of contract by the employer. The union can file a claim under the grievance and arbitration procedure without abandoning its continuing rights under the contract. The U.S. Supreme Court has stated that "Arbitration provisions, which themselves have not been repudiated, are meant to survive breaches of contract, in many contracts even total breach . . ." (*Drake Bakeries v. Local 50, American Bakery & Confectionery Workers,* 370 U.S. 254 (1962)).

**Brief**   A written statement in support of a party's position, submitted to an arbitrator either before or after the hearing. In labor arbitration, briefs are generally used to cite court decisions, prior awards, and contract language.

**Challenge of Arbitrator**   A party in arbitration can challenge the impartiality of an arbitrator, with the aim of blocking the appointment or removing the arbitrator from office. This right is afforded by section 17 of the Voluntary Labor Arbitration Rules of the AAA. In practice, such challenges seldom occur in labor arbitration because parties know the arbitrators and participate in the selection process.

**Closing Argument**   A statement customarily made by each party at the close of an arbitration hearing. The arbitrator will always allow the parties to make such summations if they so desire, but can impose time limitations. Parties frequently use the closing argument to emphasize the points upon which they base their case. Such a presentation leaves their position fresh in the mind of the arbitrator.

**Collective Bargaining**   Negotiation between an employer and an organization representing a bargaining unit of workers to create or make changes in a contract concerning the terms and conditions of employment. Once negotiated and set down in writing, this contract becomes a collective bargaining agreement. In such agreements, the arrangement for settling disputes concerning the interpretation or application of contract provisions is most frequently a grievance and arbitration procedure.

**Compensation of Arbitrator**   The fee the arbitrator receives as remuneration for services rendered. Labor arbitrators in the United States are usually paid on a *per diem* basis, with reimbursement for travel expenses. The parties generally share such costs equally. When a list is sent to the parties by the AAA, the arbitrator's *per diem* is disclosed. The arbitrator charges the parties for the entire time spent on their case. Under the expedited procedures of the AAA, labor arbitrators charge only for the hearing day, substantially reducing the overall cost.

**Compulsory Arbitration**   A system under which parties are compelled by law to arbitrate their dispute, sometimes found in statutes relating to bargaining impasses in the public sector. Laws in several states have adopted various forms of compulsory arbitration for employee groups such as police and firefighters.

**Concurrent Jurisdiction**   A situation in which one of the parties may be authorized to seek a remedy from the courts, from the National Labor Relations Board, or from arbitration. For example, both the collective bargaining agreement and the National Labor Relations Act may protect related rights. If a worker is discharged without just cause, the grievance can be arbitrated. But if discharged for union activities, the employee may have a right to file an unfair labor practice charge with the NLRB. A question may arise as to which tribunal should have primary jurisdiction. To cope with this conflict, the NLRB has determined, in the *Collyer* case (1971), that the Board will withhold its jurisdiction in favor of arbitration if certain conditions exist. Where an award has been rendered on such a case by an arbitrator, the NLRB may defer to it.

**Confirming the Award**   A labor arbitrator's award can be converted into a judgment by a court. To complete this process, the winning party must make a motion before the court to have the award confirmed. If all legal requirements have been met, the court will enter judgment. This procedure is seldom necessary in labor arbitration, where parties customarily comply with the requirements set forth in the award.

**Death of an Arbitrator**   If a neutral arbitrator dies after being appointed, a successor must be selected mutually by the parties involved or by the appointing administrative agency. Section 18 of the Voluntary Labor Arbitration Rules provides for the replacement of an arbitrator.

**Default**   Under section 27 of the AAA Voluntary Labor Arbitration Rules, an award may not be entered solely upon default. If a party fails to appear at an arbitration hearing after due notice, the arbitrator may hear testimony and render an *ex parte* award. The arbitrator must require the party present to submit proof. Such an award can then be enforced in court.

**Delegation of Arbitrator's Authority**   The authority of an arbitrator to decide a case cannot be delegated without the consent of both parties. The arbitrator should obtain the written agreement of the parties if it becomes necessary to consult outside experts to verify certain facts. The parties rely on the arbitrator's ability to understand the case and to exercise personal judgment, not on the expertise of another person. This subject is dealt with in the Code of Professional Responsibility.

**Delivery of Award** The award is usually mailed to the parties at their last known address by a representative of the AAA or by the arbitrator. If there is no contrary provision in the arbitration clause of the contract or in the applicable rules, the award can be delivered personally or sent by registered or certified mail, or in any other manner prescribed by law.

**Demand for Arbitration** The initial notice by one party to the other of an intention to arbitrate under the arbitration clause in their contract. This document may be in the form of a letter, as long as it contains the required information. The demand should identify and describe the grievance. It should contain the names of the grievant, the union, and the employer, a copy of the arbitration clause, and a statement of the remedy or relief being sought. A copy of the demand should be sent to the opposing party, and another filed with the AAA.

**Deposition** The taking of testimony under oath, to be used as evidence in an arbitration. Although arbitrators can order that such depositions be taken, the procedure is seldom necessary in labor arbitration. Testimony is given more weight if it is presented by the witness in person.

**Discovery** A procedure invoked before a court trial to inform a party of the facts in a dispute in order to facilitate preparation of the attorney's case. Discovery is seldom used in labor arbitration, where both parties have participated in the earlier grievance procedure. In rare situations, it may be necessary. In these cases, discovery can be encouraged by the arbitrator.

**Disqualification of Arbitrator**   An arbitrator can be disqualified for misconduct. The fact that an arbitrator failed to disclose a personal relationship with a lawyer for one of the parties might constitute sufficient grounds for disqualification. If the other party knows of the relationship and fails to object, however, it may have waived the right to challenge the award.

**Duty of Fair Representation**   The obligation of a union to safeguard the rights of all members of the bargaining unit. This duty is imposed by federal labor law. Some union constitutions provide remedies for members who are dissatisfied with the handling of their grievances. The union's duty to represent its members in a fair manner does not require that every grievance be carried to arbitration. In the event of a failure to provide fair representation, both the union and the employer may be liable.

**Duty to Disclose**   The arbitrator must reveal any fact or circumstance that might make it difficult to render a fair and just award. When notified of selection, the arbitrator should disclose anything of this nature. If anything develops later which was not previously known, the arbitrator should reveal it at once to the AAA administrator or to the parties. See the Code of Professional Responsibility.

**Enforcement of Arbitration Agreements**   Courts customarily enforce agreements to arbitrate. The most influential decision is *Textile Workers Union v. Lincoln Mills* (1957), where the U.S. Supreme Court enforced an arbitration clause in a collective bargaining agreement, finding legislative support in Section 301 of the Taft–Hartley Act.

**Examination before Trial**  Most authorities consider this procedure to be incompatible with labor arbitration, wherein the grievance procedure gives both parties a prior opportunity to determine the circumstances of the case and to confront witnesses.

**Exclusionary Clause**  A provision in the collective bargaining agreement that excludes specific subjects from the arbitration process.

**Execution of Award**  The signing of an award by the arbitrator, with whatever formalities may be required by law. Statutes differ as to requirements. In some jurisdictions, the signature must be acknowledged. These technical requirements are known to each AAA regional office, so that awards issued in that state can be put in proper form.

**Expert Witness**  A person with special skills or experience in a profession or with a recognized knowledge of a technical area.

**Federal Mediation and Conciliation Service (FMCS)**  An independent agency of the federal government, established under Title II of the Labor–Management Relations Act of 1947, to mediate and conciliate labor disputes in any industry affecting commerce, other than the railroad and air transportation industries. One of the major responsibilities imposed on the FMCS by the Labor–Management Relations Act of 1947 is the prevention of labor–management disputes. The FMCS provides government facilities for labor contract mediation.

***Functus Officio***  The doctrine of *functus officio*, as applied to arbitration, recognizes the termination of an *ad* *hoc* arbitrator's authority after rendering the award. Under most laws, only the parties or a reviewing court can authorize resubmission to the original arbitrator.

**Grievance**   A complaint against an employer, made on behalf of an employee by the union representative, alleging failure to comply with the obligations of the collective bargaining contract. The grievance may result from disciplinary action against the employee. Any complaint relating to an employee's pay, working conditions, or contract interpretation is generally considered to be a grievance.

**Grievance Arbitration**   The submission of labor grievances to an impartial arbitrator for final determination. Sometimes called "arbitration of rights." Grievances may involve a wide variety of issues. The arbitrator determines the meaning of the contract and clarifies and interprets its terms. Jurisdiction of the arbitrator is sometimes restricted to those disputes that involve the interpretation or application of the contract. Increasingly, arbitrators are required to resolve issues involving the application of various public labor laws, such as unfair labor practices and charges of employment discrimination. Arbitration, in most contracts, is the last step in the grievance procedure.

**Grievance Procedure**   The steps established in a collective bargaining contract for the handling of complaints made on behalf of employees. A grievance procedure provides a means by which a union or an individual employee can submit a complaint, without disrupting the production process or endangering the employee's job. The primary intent is to settle the dispute as soon as possible.

These procedural steps vary from contract to contract. For example, a grievance may be taken by the shop steward of the aggrieved employee to the supervisor. If no settlement is reached, it may be appealed through successive steps. The grievant may be represented by various union officials. Smaller companies tend to have shorter grievance procedures, consisting of two or three steps. In larger companies, or in multiplant contracts, there may be grievance committees with union–management representation, followed by joint boards. These systems should be reviewed from time to time to ensure that they are functioning properly.

**Hearing**   The presentation of a case in arbitration. The fundamental requirements for a valid hearing are that the arbitrator be present, that the persons whose rights are affected be given notice of the proceedings, and that the parties be heard and allowed to present all relevant and material evidence and to cross-examine witnesses appearing against them. These rights are fully protected in the Voluntary Labor Arbitration Rules of the AAA.

**Impartial Chairperson**   An arbitrator who is the impartial member of an arbitration board. Such a chairperson may be appointed for the duration of the contract, in which case he or she is called a permanent chairperson. The term is also used to designate the neutral member of an *ad hoc* arbitration board chosen by mutual consent of the parties. In such a case, the other members of the tribunal may be party-appointed arbitrators, each having been chosen by one of the parties. It is usually understood that such persons are partisan.

**Impasse**   A deadlock in negotiations. When collective

bargaining has failed to produce an agreement between the parties, they must decide whether to bargain further. Sometimes a strike is called to produce pressure for a settlement.

In some cases, the parties are willing to use arbitration to help resolve some of the remaining issues. And in public employment, laws are being passed to require that the parties use a variety of settlement techniques, including mediation, factfinding (with or without the power to make recommendations for settlement), cooling-off periods with various time limits enforceable by court injunction, and final and binding compulsory arbitration.

**Individual Rights**   The rights that individual employees retain despite the designation of a union as their exclusive bargaining agent. An employee can sue the union if it has failed to provide fair representation, but the employee rarely has an absolute right to have a personal grievance taken to arbitration. Although the union represents all employees, union interests rest with the majority. The union must be free to decide which grievances should be pursued.

**Injunction**   A court order restraining a person or an organization from performing an act that would result in serious injury to the rights of another person or group. An injunction may require a specific action. Any violation of an injunction is punishable as contempt of court. In rare instances, injunctions may be used to order a union not to strike. They were issued more often before the passage of the Norris–LaGuardia Act in 1932, which limited the powers of federal courts to issue injunctions. A number of states adopted similar statutes. Injunctions can also be used in national emergency disputes under the

Taft–Hartley Act, postponing a strike for a period of up to 80 days.

Following the *Boys Markets* ruling, courts have been given the power to enjoin wildcat strikes in situations where the union has committed itself to arbitration.

Though injunctive relief is seldom used, some collective agreements give an arbitrator the power to hold an expedited hearing when a claim is made that the no-strike or no-lockout clause has been violated. If the claim is found to be valid, the arbitrator may enjoin the violation.

**Interest Arbitration**   Arbitration of the terms of a collective bargaining contract. When contract negotiations reach an impasse and cannot be resolved by collective bargaining, the issues in dispute can be submitted to voluntary arbitration. Several industries have traditionally included provisions for arbitrating new terms in their contracts. Even after a strike, the parties may resort to voluntary arbitration. Although unions and employers have been reluctant to accept arbitration as a means of settling interest disputes, in recent years there has been renewed interest in the idea.

**Interim Award**   Most arbitration statutes in the United States require that arbitration awards be final and that they determine all of the issues submitted. But where the parties have given expressed or implied consent for an interim award, arbitrators may be authorized to determine some but not all of the issues. Interim awards are sometimes rendered by labor arbitrators in situations where further studies must be made by the parties before the remaining issues can be determined.

**Judicial Notice**   The recognition by a labor arbitrator that certain facts in a case are self-evident or of common knowledge. Arbitrators may recognize laws of other jurisdictions, official acts of government agencies, common practices in collective bargaining, and similar facts that are so well known that there should be no burden of having to establish them by proof.

**Jurisdiction**   The legal power or right to exercise authority. The jurisdiction of a labor arbitrator is defined and limited by agreement of the parties. From time to time, it has been necessary for courts to decide whether the issues in a dispute lie within the jurisdiction of the arbitrator. But this issue can also be submitted for determination by the arbitrator.

**Labor Dispute**   A disagreement between parties to a collective bargaining agreement over the terms (interests) or the interpretation of the terms (rights) of their contract. The Norris–LaGuardia Act of March 23, 1932, at § 13(c), defines a labor dispute as follows: "The term 'labor dispute' includes any controversy concerning terms or conditions of employment, or concerning the association or representation of persons in negotiating, fixing, maintaining, changing, or seeking to arrange terms or conditions of employment, regardless of whether or not the disputants stand in the proximate relation of employer and employee."

**Laches**   Unreasonable delay in asserting a right which might prevent its enforcement. Arbitrators may consider laches when selecting a remedy to a dispute. An arbitrator might rule that a party who has "slept on its claimed rights" for too long has lost its claim.

**Liability of Arbitrator**   A labor arbitrator is immune from civil or legal action for any award, nor is an arbitrator required to explain the reasons for the award or to testify about the case. Without such immunity, arbitrators would be vulnerable to lawsuits from losing parties.

**Locale of Arbitration**  The city where the arbitration is held. In labor arbitration, hearings are generally held at a place that is convenient for the union and the employer, often the plant or a nearby hotel. Reference to AAA rules in the contract permits the AAA to fix the locale when the parties cannot agree. When appointed, the arbitrator can decide where and when the hearing is to be held, in accordance with the mutual convenience and desires of the parties.

**Management Rights**  Clauses often appear in collective bargaining contracts that establish management's right to operate the business. Many labor arbitration cases have involved the definition of "management rights." Some contracts go into great detail in specifying these rights. Disputes nevertheless arise as to whether those rights have been exercised reasonably or whether they have been abandoned.

**Mediation**  Participation by a third party in negotiations for the purpose of helping the parties resolve their disagreement. The success of this technique often depends on the skill of the mediator. The mediator might meet with the parties separately or arrange joint conferences. The mediator tries to facilitate the bargaining process by clarifying the issues and helping the parties to discover areas of possible compromise. The mediator can offer suggestions, but cannot force either party to accept a solution. The mediator may sometimes recommend that the parties agree to arbitrate those issues not settled by mediation.

**Merging Seniority Lists** The combining of seniority lists when plants or departments within a company consolidate. Various methods for resolving such seniority issues have been developed, involving principles such as length of service, follow the work, or the surviving group. An increasing number of recent cases have involved mergers intended to eliminate "islands of discrimination."

**Merits of a Case** The substantive issues involved in an arbitration case. In its *Steelworkers' Trilogy* decisions, the U.S. Supreme Court ruled that judges are not to consider the merits of a case when determining arbitrability or enforcement. Judges should not substitute their judgment for that of the arbitrator.

**Modifying the Award** In labor arbitration, the arbitrator's award is the terminal point in the resolution of a grievance. Courts are hesitant to order a rehearing by the arbitrator or to modify or correct the award. Some arbitration statutes authorize the arbitrator to correct miscalculations of figures or mistakes in the identification of the parties. But in correcting such errors, the arbitrator cannot reexamine the merits of the decision.

**Motion to Compel Arbitration** A form of legal action used by the moving party to petition a court to compel the other party to arbitrate. Where a motion to compel is deemed necessary, supporting affidavits and documents should provide evidence that there is an agreement to arbitrate, that a dispute exists, and that the opposing party has refused to arbitrate. The court cannot consider the merits of the controversy.

**Multiple Grievances** The filing of two or more unrelated grievances by a union, to be heard in a single hearing before the same arbitrator. The union's right to file multiple grievances depends upon contract language and past practice.

**National Academy of Arbitrators**  An organization founded in 1947 to foster high standards of knowledge and skill on a professional level among those engaged in the arbitration of industrial disputes. The National Academy is not an agency for the selection or appointment of arbitrators. At its annual meeting, lectures on various aspects of arbitration are delivered, which are published by the Bureau of National Affairs under the title, "Proceedings of the Annual Meeting of the National Academy of Arbitrators."

**National Labor Relations Board (NLRB)**  An independent federal agency created by Congress in 1935 to administer the National Labor Relations Act of July 5, 1935. Under the National Labor Relations Act, as amended in 1947 by the Taft–Hartley Act, the NLRB has two primary functions: first, to determine through agency-conducted secret ballot elections which union is to be the exclusive representative of employees for the purpose of collective bargaining; and, second, to prevent and remedy unfair labor practices by both labor organizations and employers. Whenever appropriate, the Board will defer to the parties' existing grievance and arbitration procedures in situations where both contractual and unfair labor practice rights are involved.

**National Panel of Labor Arbitrators**  A list of some 3,500 persons skilled in labor arbitration who are available through the nationwide network of AAA offices to serve as arbitrators throughout the United States. Arbitrators are carefully screened by the AAA for expertise and impartiality before being appointed to the panel.

**No-Strike Clause**   A clause in a collective bargaining contract under which a union agrees that it will not strike during the life of the contract. In 1957, the U.S. Supreme Court held, in *Lincoln Mills,* that an agreement to arbitrate grievances in a collective bargaining agreement is the "quid pro quo" for a union's promise not to strike.

**Notice of Hearing**   Formal notification of the time and place of a hearing. The rules of the AAA provide that an arbitrator can fix the time and place for each hearing. In so doing, the arbitrator respects the mutual convenience and desires of the parties. Under AAA rules, such a notice must be mailed at least five days in advance.

**Open-End Grievance Procedure**   A grievance procedure which has as its final step the right to strike. Such agreements are increasingly rare. Most contracts provide for final and binding arbitration.

**Opening Statement**   Brief remarks made at the opening of a hearing by each advocate, intended to inform the arbitrator of the nature of the dispute and of the evidence they intend to present. It is usual for the claimant to be heard first, but the arbitrator may vary the order.

**Opinion**   A written document in which the arbitrator sets forth the reasons for the award. In most labor cases, the parties want the arbitrator to explain the reasoning in order to give them some guidance for similar situations that might arise under the contract. But in other situations the parties can ask the AAA to notify the arbitrator that no opinion will be required. This can substantially reduce the cost and delay of arbitration.

**Party-Appointed Arbitrator**   An arbitrator chosen by one of the parties. It is common for such arbitrators to act in a partisan manner. Party-appointed arbitrators are being used less frequently in labor arbitration as the many ambiguities and problems created by their participation are recognized. Most modern grievance arbitration systems provide for a single, neutral arbitrator.

**Past Practice**   A course of action knowingly followed by a union and a company over a period of time. Where such a pattern exists, the workers involved come to regard it as normal. Past practice becomes significant in arbitration whenever one of the parties submits evidence of it to support its claim. In the *Warrior & Gulf* case, Justice Douglas stated: "The labor arbitrator's source of law is not confined to the express provisions of the contract, as the industrial common law—the practices of the industry and the shop—is equally a part of the collective bargaining agreement although not expressed in it."

**Permanent Arbitrator**   An arbitrator who is selected to serve under the terms of a collective bargaining agreement for a specified period of time or for the life of the contract. The duties of a permanent arbitrator are defined in the contract.

**Precedent**   The concept that prior decisions serve as a rule that must be followed. Prior opinions are not binding on a labor arbitrator even though they may be considered in determining the case. Prior decisions on the same point may, of course, be treated as precedent by the parties. This is often done in permanent-umpire systems. But the general rule in *ad hoc* arbitration is that the arbitrator is not bound by earlier decisions on the same issue. On the other hand, the arbitrator will often find such opinions relevant to the case under consideration.

**Prehearing Conference**   A meeting of the arbitrator or an AAA representative with the parties, prior to the actual hearing, in order to establish appropriate procedural groundrules or to identify the issues to be determined. Such conferences are seldom necessary in labor arbitration cases. Ordinarily, the grievance procedure has afforded the parties ample opportunity to become familiar with the case and to attempt to settle it. It is customary for arbitrators to encounter the issues for the first time at the initial hearing.

**Public Employee**   A person who is employed by a municipal, county, state, or federal agency. Public employees are subject to various public employment relations laws that generally have the effect of restricting their freedom to engage in work stoppages, often by replacing the right to strike with various impasse settlement mechanisms.

**Recognition Clause**   A clause in collective bargaining contracts that commits the employer to deal with the named union as the bargaining agent for the employees in the unit. The National Labor Relations Act requires an employer to recognize the union that represents a majority of the employees in an appropriate bargaining unit.

**Reinstatement**   The return of a discharged employee to the job. The crucial issue in discharge cases is whether the discharge was for just cause and whether the penalty was fair and reasonable. An arbitrator may reinstate an employee with full pay for the time lost, reduce such back pay by various amounts, or reinstate the employee with no back pay. Under some contracts, the arbitrator's power to fashion an appropriate remedy has been limited by the parties.

**Reopening of Hearings**   A hearing may be reopened on the arbitrator's initiative or at the request of a party. The arbitrator may wish to reopen the hearings to have the parties clarify the issue or present further testimony. A party may request a reopening of hearings for the presentation of new evidence. Before granting such a request, the arbitrator should offer the opposing party the opportunity to present any objections. If reopening the hearings would delay the award beyond the 30-day time limit specified in the AAA rules, or beyond the contractual time limits, the matter may not be reopened unless both parties agree.

**Residual Rights**   The residual rights doctrine gives management the benefit of the doubt concerning rights and powers on which the contract is silent. An arbitrator will examine the contract to determine whether the employer had agreed to reduce the extent of its traditional rights.

*Res Judicata*   A legal doctrine to the effect that once an issue has been determined, it need not be litigated again. The purpose of the doctrine is to prevent repetitious lawsuits. Once a case has been properly determined in arbitration, its issues are considered to be *res judicata* with regard to the parties.

**Respondent**   In labor arbitration, this term is used for the party against whom a demand for arbitration is asserted. Ordinarily this is the employer.

**Right to Counsel**   Each party to a labor arbitration has a right to be represented by an advocate. This right is recognized in the AAA Voluntary Labor Arbitration Rules.

There is no requirement that parties be represented by an attorney. Unions and employers are sometimes represented by lay representatives experienced in labor arbitration.

**Rotating Panel**   A panel of arbitrators selected on a rotating basis for the life of the contract. By this means, parties to a contract seek to expedite the selection process while still using arbitrators who are familiar with their contract and relationship. If such rotating panels are administered by the AAA, the arbitrations can be held under its rules.

**Rules of Evidence**   Courtroom rules of evidence are not applicable in arbitration. Under AAA labor arbitration rules, the arbitrator determines whether evidence is relevant and material. The arbitrator will determine when hearsay may be admitted, when to accept a copy instead of the original document, and when to admit evidence of oral agreements. Before making a ruling on contested evidence, the arbitrator will listen to the parties' arguments on the issue. Ordinarily, labor arbitrators are willing to accept evidence submitted by either party for whatever probative value it may have; but this should not be abused. An arbitrator is unlikely to be persuaded by irrelevant or immaterial evidence, and it is unwise to try the arbitrator's patience.

**Section 301 Disputes**   Section 301 of the Taft–Hartley Act reads as follows: "Suits for violation of contracts between an employer and a labor organization representing employees in an industry affecting commerce as defined in this act, . . . may be brought in any district court of the United States having jurisdiction of the parties, without respect to the amount in controversy or without regard to the citizenship of the parties." In fact, most employers and

112

unions have inserted grievance and arbitration clauses into their contracts to eliminate the need for such litigation. The rights created by this section can be enforced in accordance with the terms of the arbitration clause in a collective bargaining contract.

**Seniority**   The relative length of service of an employee with an employer or particular seniority unit. Seniority often determines the rights of one employee in relation to others as to layoff, shift preference, promotion, vacation, severance pay, or retirement benefits. The seniority rights of an employee are defined in the collective bargaining contract.

**Statute of Limitations**   A statute that determines the time during which any claim or right is still enforceable. In labor arbitration, the term is also used loosely for the time periods contained in the collective bargaining agreement. These agreements may contain time limitations for performing various acts such as filing a grievance or appealing the decision of a company in the grievance procedure. Both courts and arbitrators vary in their treatment of such provisions. The U.S. Supreme Court in *John Wiley & Sons v. Livingston* held that it is up to the arbitrator to decide whether there was compliance with the time limits provided in the contract.

**Sufficient Ability Clause**   A clause in a labor contract creating a standard for determining which employee shall be awarded a particular job. Sufficient ability clauses create minimum acceptable qualifications for doing the work, provided the employee in question has seniority. The interpretation and application of such provisions are the source of many disputes.

**Taft–Hartley Act** (Labor Management Relations Act, Pub. L. No. 101, 80th Cong., 1st Sess.; 29 U.S.C.A. §§ 141–197) An act passed in 1947 over President Truman's veto that modified the National Labor Relations Act by restricting union activities. The Taft–Hartley Act provided special machinery for handling national emergency disputes. It established the Federal Mediation and Conciliation Service. Title 1 of the Taft–Hartley Act has had particular and specific importance for arbitration. The U.S. Supreme Court based its landmark decision in *Lincoln Mills* on this section, authorizing enforcement of an arbitration agreement and the subsequent award.

**Transcript of Hearing** A verbatim record of an arbitration hearing in the form of a stenographic report. The use of a reporter in labor arbitration is the exception rather than the rule. A transcript can be made at the request of either party. If only one party asks for a transcript, that party is obliged to pay for it. Costs are otherwise shared by both parties.

**Unfair Labor Practice** An act on the part of a union or an employer that interferes with the rights of employees to join labor unions and engage in collective bargaining. Section 8 of the National Labor Relations Act makes such conduct unlawful and empowers the National Labor Relations Board to prevent or remedy it. State statutes may also declare certain acts to be unfair labor practices. Arbitrators have no jurisdiction over unfair labor practices except in those cases where such practices also violate collective bargaining agreements.

# Court and NLRB Decisions that Have Contributed to the Language of Labor–Management Arbitration

*Spielberg Manufacturing Co.*, 112 NLRB 1080 (1955) [*Spielberg Doctrine*]. The Taft–Hartley Act forbids discrimination against employees for union activities, as do virtually all collective bargaining contracts. Thus, when an employee or union accuses an employer of so discriminating, both a contractual and a statutory violation are involved. If a contractual remedy is pursued, does this foreclose the claimant from later pursuing the statutory remedy? In 1955, the NLRB ruled that it would defer to arbitration provided basic safeguards were met. In general, the arbitration had to be fair, and the same issue that would be presented to the NLRB had to have been considered by the arbitrator. Courts have upheld the Board's right to decline to rule on "dual jurisdiction" cases under such circumstances.

*Textile Workers Union of America v. Lincoln Mills*, 353 U.S. 448 (1957). The United States Supreme Court ruled that future dispute clauses in collective bargaining agreements in industries affecting interstate commerce can be enforced in federal courts under section 301(a) of the Taft–Hartley Act. Writing for the majority, Justice William O. Douglas said that the agreement to arbitrate grievance disputes "is the *quid pro quo* for an agreement not to strike." For that reason, he said, section 301 should be thought of as conferring federal jurisdiction for the purpose of invoking a remedy for a failure by a party to honor its agreement to arbitrate. Although this decision was narrow in many respects, it formed the basis for establishing the jurisdiction of federal courts in labor matters and led to further important decisions, notably the three cases often referred to as the *Steelworkers' Trilogy*, decided by the U.S. Supreme Court on June 20, 1960.

*United Steelworkers of America v. Warrior & Gulf Navigation Co.*, 363 U.S. 574 (1960). By this decision, and by its decision in *United Steelworkers of America v. American Manufacturing Co.*, 363 U.S. 564 (1960) (the second of the three *Steelworkers' Trilogy* cases), the court struck down a practice in some lower courts of refusing enforcement of arbitration agreements merely because the grievance seemed to be lacking in merit. It was held that the courts should resolve disputes over arbitrability in favor of coverage unless it could be said "with positive assurance" that the parties excluded the issue from the scope of their arbitration clauses.

*United Steelworkers of America v. Enterprise Wheel & Car Corp.*, 363 U.S. 593 (1960). This was the third decision in the *Trilogy*. The effect of this ruling was to uphold the arbitrator's authority to remedy violations of collective bargaining agreements. "When an arbitrator is commissioned to interpret and apply the collective bargaining agreement," the court wrote, "he is to bring his informed judgment to bear in order to reach a fair solution of a problem. This is especially true when it comes to formulating remedies. There is a need for flexibility in meeting a wide variety of situations."

*John Wiley & Sons, Inc. v. Livingston*, 376 U.S. 543 (1964). This U.S. Supreme Court case involved many complicated issues, but centered on whether a collective bargaining agreement survived the purchase of a company by a firm whose employees were not organized. An important part of the decision held that procedural arbitrability (whether time limits and other conditions precedent to arbitration have been complied with) are matters for the arbitrator to determine. This case is distinguishable from *Warrior & Gulf*, where it was held that substantive issues of arbitrability can be determined by the courts.

*Boys Markets, Inc. v. Retail Clerks Union*, 398 U.S. 239 (1970). The U.S. Supreme Court decided that an award enjoining a strike in violation of a collective bargaining agreement is enforceable, notwithstanding the Norris–LaGuardia Act's proscription of injunctions in labor disputes.

*Collyer Insulated Wire*, 192 NLRB 837 (1971). The NLRB withheld jurisdiction when the issues involved could be determined under an arbitration clause, subject to the matter being resubmitted for further review after being determined in the grievance procedure or pursuant to an arbitrator's award.

*Alexander v. Gardner–Denver Co.*, 415 U.S. 36 (1974). This case involved the treatment of Title VII rights of the individual employee. The U.S. Supreme Court held that an employee's right to a trial *de novo* of a claim of race or sex discrimination is not foreclosed by an unfavorable arbitration award under the nondiscrimination clause, but the trial judge should give "great weight" to the arbitrator's decision.

*Bowen v. United States Postal Service*, 459 U.S. 12 (1983). The U.S. Supreme Court held that a union is responsible for the increase in damages to a grievant resulting from breach of its duty of fair representation in failing to process a grievance through arbitration. "To require the union to pay damages does not impose a burden on the union inconsistent with the national labor policy, but rather provides an additional incentive for the union to process its members' claims where warranted." This clarified the earlier decisions in *Vaca v. Sipes*, 386 U.S. 171 (1967), and *Hines v. Anchor Motor Freight, Inc.*, 424 U.S. 554 (1976).

*W. R. Grace & Co. v. Local 759, Rubber Workers*, 461 U.S. 757 (1983). The role of a court in reviewing an arbitration award is limited to whether the award drew its essence from the collective bargaining agreement. If so, the award must be upheld unless it violates public policy. In the instant case, an arbitrator's upholding of the contractual seniority provisions, despite the company having entered into an Equal Employment Opportunity Commission conciliation agreement to retain certain junior employees in a layoff situation, did not serve to compromise public policy favoring voluntary compliance with Title VII. Therefore, the arbitration award was held enforceable by the U.S. Supreme Court.

*DelCostello v. Int'l Brotherhood of Teamsters*, 462 U.S. 151 (1983). In a consolidation of two separate duty of fair representation claims, the U.S. Supreme Court overturned its decision in *United Parcel Service, Inc. v. Mitchell*, 451

U.S. 56 (1981), and ruled that no available state statutes adequately served to balance the rights of the aggrieved employee and the union and employer. The Court thus chose the federal six-month statute of limitations for unfair labor practice charges over state statutes providing for longer time limits, stating that the application of a federal limitations period to such suits would provide a better balancing of interests.

*McDonald v. City of West Branch, Michigan,* 466 U.S. 284 (1984). In this case, the U.S. Supreme Court once again determined that an employee's claims based on statutory rights are not finally foreclosed by a grievance arbitration award. The Court held that in an action brought under the Civil Rights Act, a federal court should not give binding effect to an arbitration award made pursuant to a collective bargaining agreement, ruling that the plain language of the federal statute, which specifies that *judicial proceedings* are to be given full faith and credit, did not apply to arbitration.

*Allis-Chalmers Corp. v. Lueck,* 471 U.S. 202 (1985). The Supreme Court ruled that where a claim is asserted under state law but is based on interpretation of the collective bargaining agreement, state law is preempted by federal labor law, and the claim must be dismissed if the employee failed to pursue the contract grievance procedure. The Court stated that a "rule that permitted an individual to sidestep available grievance procedures would cause arbitration to lose much of its effectiveness,... as well as eviscerate a central tenet of federal labor-contract law under § 301 that it is the arbitrator, not the court, who has the responsibility to interpret the labor contract in the first instance."

*Cornelius v. Nutt*, 472 U.S. 648 (1985). The Civil Service Reform Act of 1978 provides that federal employees may appeal disciplinary actions to the Merit Systems Protection Board, which is empowered to overturn the disciplinary action if the employee successfully proves that he or she was prejudiced by "harmful error" in the application of the agency's disciplinary procedures. Those federal employees who are also members of a union may have the option of choosing to grieve the disciplinary action through their union. The question before the U.S. Supreme Court was whether an arbitrator, finding no prejudice to the individual employee due to "harmful error" but finding prejudice to the union, could overturn disciplinary action taken against the individual employee. The Court ruled that an arbitrator must apply the same statutory review standards as the Board, to prevent forum shopping and avoid inconsistent results.

*AT&T Technologies, Inc. v. Communications Workers of America*, 475 U.S. 643 (1986). The U.S. Supreme Court reversed the district court's ruling that the question of arbitrability was for the arbitrator. Reaffirming its position in the *Steelworkers' Trilogy*, the Court ruled that arbitrability is unquestionably a matter for judicial determination: "It is the court's duty to interpret the agreement and to determine whether the parties intended to arbitrate grievances concerning layoffs predicated on a 'lack of work' determination by the Company. If the court determines that the agreement so provides, then it is for the arbitrator to determine the relative agreement. It was for the court, not the arbitrator, to decide in the first instance whether the dispute was to be resolved through arbitration." The case was remanded for a determination of arbitrability.

*Chicago Teachers Union Local 1 v. Hudson*, 475 U.S. 292 (1986). The U.S. Supreme Court affirmed the Seventh Circuit's finding that a union's agency shop fee procedures were constitutionally inadequate. It found that the procedures had three fundamental flaws: (1) the mere offer of a possible dues rebate did not guarantee that nonmembers' fees would not be used for impermissible purposes; (2) the information disseminated on how the agency shop fee was calculated was inadequate; and (3) the dispute resolution procedure, entirely under the union's control, failed to provide for quick, impartial decision making.

*United Paperworkers International Union, AFL-CIO v. Misco, Inc.*, 108 S. Ct. 364 (1987). The U.S. Supreme Court reversed the judgment of the Fifth Circuit and held that the court erred in setting aside an arbitral award on public policy grounds. It found that the court inappropriately drew an inference that was outside of the limited scope of judicial review and failed to show that the alleged public policy violation was "well defined and dominant" and based on more than just "general considerations of supposed public interests." The Supreme Court further reaffirmed an important principle of arbitration law—namely that, absent proof of fraud or dishonesty, courts may not review the merits of an arbitration award.

*Lingle v. Norge Division of Magic Chef, Inc.*, 486 U.S. 399 (1988). Where an employee is covered by a collective bargaining agreement (CBA) that provides a contractual remedy for discharge without just cause, a state law remedy for retaliatory discharge may still be enforced as long as the application of state law does not require interpretation of the CBA.

# The Arbitrator's Alphabet

For the guidance of practitioners, we have included the following material that describes some of the attributes that parties find objectionable in some arbitrators.

**A.** Parties don't like an ADVOCATE who tries to "make a case" for one of the parties. No union official likes to be embarrassed in front of the membership.

**B.** Nor do they want an arbitrator who is a BULLY. Arbitrators should not heckle a witness. They resent it when an arbitrator takes over their case, telling them what questions to ask and what points to argue.

**C.** Most important the arbitrator should not be CROOKED. Honesty is essential since the process is based upon trust.

**D.** The parties want an arbitrator who will listen to their case, not one who is constantly DEBATING the issues.

**E.** The arbitrator should not be such an EGOTIST that it is no longer possible to insert a new idea in his or her head.

**F.** They don't want a FERRET who would carry on an independent examination, probing for possible collusion, suspecting their motivations, or "running barefoot through their contract" looking for new legal theories. They want the arbitrator to listen and to try to decide the case in a reasonable fashion.

**G.** The arbitrator shouldn't play GOD, attempting to

administer universal justice based on some unknown theory of morality. The four corners of the contract and generally accepted standards of just cause provide appropriate guidelines for the arbitrator.

**H.** There may be some humorous aspects to the situation, but the arbitrator should not try to be a HUMORIST. A grievance is a serious matter. The arbitrator should not make fun of the grievant or the supervisor in the award. Ridicule is seldom appreciated by the people in the plant.

**I.** Nor do they want an INVENTOR who would try to create a better remedy than management had imposed. The duty of the arbitrator is to decide, not to create a new dispute.

**J.** They don't want a JURIST. They like arbitration because it is informal. Neither the company nor the business agent want to wrangle about the burden of proof or the rules of evidence. Arbitration avoids legalisms. Precedents can be useful. But they want the arbitrator to decide based on the facts of their case. The parties have to pay for an arbitrator's study time. They are not interested in supporting the arbitrator's scholarship.

**K.** The parties don't want an arbitrator who runs a KANGAROO COURT. They want a fair hearing.

**L.** Having worked out the terms of their own collective bargaining contract, they don't want a LEGISLATOR who attempts to amend their agreement to suit his or her own brand of industrial justice.

**M.** Nor do they want a MEDIATOR who will try to pressure them to compromise the case. They don't mind being encouraged to stipulate some of the facts, but they do not want to be pressured to settle.

**N.** They will avoid a NITPICKER who would make them review the entire working history of the company.

**O.** They hope that the arbitrator will not be an OVER-CHARGER, flying first class, staying at expensive hotels, and billing them for champagne and caviar, while spending unnecessary time researching the common law of "just cause."

**P.** They don't want a PREACHER as an arbitrator. They hope that the award will limit itself to the issue and will not include any sermonizing on the morality in the plant. They don't want an arbitrator who will lay the foundation for a Title VII claim.

**Q.** The arbitrator should have no QUALMS about deciding their case.

**R.** Nor are they looking for a REFORMER, an arbitrator who views his or her role as a social worker or psychiatrist trying to protect the grievant against a grasping capitalistic system. Nor do they want an arbitrator who would suggest that the grievant was not adequately represented by the union.

**S.** They don't want an arbitrator who is SENILE. Some arbitrators lose their wits at fifty; others are sharp at eighty. Intelligence and good judgment are essential for an arbitrator.

**T.** The arbitrator should not be TARDY, either in showing up at the hearing or in issuing the award.

**U.** The arbitrator should never be UNCONSCIOUS, falling asleep or losing track of what is being said; close attention is required at all times. A clear head and an open mind is what the parties want.

**V.** They don't want an arbitrator who is VAGUE about the rules. If not experienced, the arbitrator should at least give the impression of being experienced.

**W.** And there are other kinds of WEAKLINGS that they don't want: arbitrators who try to make friends with everyone so that they will be picked again; arbitrators who can't make a ruling, taking testimony for "what it is worth"; and arbitrators who can't turn down a free meal from one of the parties. They prefer to deal with arbitrators who are strong and independent.

**X.** An arbitrator should be impartial and should avoid *EX PARTE* discussions of the case. The arbitrator should abide by the Code of Professional Responsibility.

**Y.** They don't want a YOUNGSTER, someone with no experience in labor relations.

**Z.** Nor do they want a ZANY. It is all right to be mildly eccentric, but not ludicrously insane.

# Basic References on Labor Arbitration

## Public and Private Sectors

Arnold, Selma, ed. *Basic Labor Relations.* New York: Practising Law Institute, 1976.

Baderschneider, Earl R., and Paul F. Miller, eds. *Labor Arbitration in Health Care: A Case Book.* New York: Spectrum Publications, 1976.

Baer, Walter E. *Discipline and Discharge under the Labor Agreement.* New York: American Management Association, 1972.

———. *The Labor Arbitration Guide.* Homewood, Ill.: Dow Jones–Irwin, 1974.

———. *Winning in Labor Arbitration.* Chicago: Crain Books, 1982.

Beeler, Duane. *Arbitration for the Local Union.* Chicago: Union Representative, 1977.

Blockhaus, Arthur P. *Grievance Arbitration Case Studies.* Boston: Cahners Books, 1974.

Bowers, Mollie H. *Contract Administration in the Public Sector.* Public Employee Relations Library, 53. Chicago: International Personnel Management Association, 1976.

Colosi, Thomas R., and Arthur Eliot Berkeley. *Collective Bargaining: How It Works and Why.* New York: American Arbitration Association, 1986.

Coulson, Robert. *Alcohol, Drugs, and Arbitration.* New York: American Arbitration Association, 1987.

———. *Arbitration in the Schools: An Analysis of Fifty-Nine Grievance Arbitration Cases.* New York: American Arbitration Association, 1986.

———. *The Termination Handbook.* New York: Free Press, 1981.

Edmonson, William Fred. *Grievance Arbitration and Its Role in the Settlement of Professional Negotiation Disputes in Higher Education.* Ann Arbor: University Microfilms International, 1980.

Elkouri, Frank, and Edna Asper Elkouri. *How Arbitration Works.* 4th ed. Washington, D.C.: Bureau of National Affairs, 1985.

Fairweather, Owen. *Practice and Procedure in Labor Arbitration.* 2d ed. Washington, D.C.: Bureau of National Affairs, 1983.

Feuille, Peter. *Final Offer Arbitration: Concepts, Developments, Techniques.* Chicago: International Personnel Management Association, 1975.

Fleming, Robben Wright. *The Labor Arbitration Process.* Urbana: University of Illinois Press, 1965.

Gilroy, Thomas P., and Russel R. Dafflitto. *Preparation and Presentation of Interest Arbitration Cases.* Iowa City: Center of Labor and Management, College of Administration, University of Iowa, 1975.

*Grievance Guide.* 6th ed. Washington, D.C.: Bureau of National Affairs, 1982.

Harrison, Allan J. *Preparing and Presenting Your Arbitration Case: A Manual for Union and Management Representatives.* Washington, D.C.: Bureau of National Affairs, 1979.

Hill, Marvin F., Jr., and Anthony V. Sinicropi. *Evidence in Arbitration.* 2d ed. Washington, D.C.: Bureau of National Affairs, 1987.

———. *Management Rights: A Legal and Arbitral Analysis.* Washington, D.C.: Bureau of National Affairs, 1986.

International Labour Office. *Grievance Arbitration: A Practical Guide.* Geneva: 1977.

Kagel, Sam. *Anatomy of a Labor Arbitration.* 2d ed. Washington, D.C.: Bureau of National Affairs, 1986.

Kershen, Harry, ed. *Impasse and Grievance Resolution.* Farmingdale, N.Y.: Baywood Publishing Company, 1976.

Kochan, Thomas A., *et al. Dispute Resolution under Fact-Finding and Arbitration: An Empirical Analysis.* New York: American Arbitration Association, 1979.

Koven, Adolph M., and Susan L. Smith. *Just Cause: The Seven Tests.* San Francisco: Coloracre Publications, Inc., 1985.

Levin, Edward, and Donald Grody. *Witnesses in Arbitration.* Washington, D.C.: Bureau of National Affairs, 1987.

Levin, Noel Arnold, ed. *Arbitrating Labor Cases.* Corporate Law and Practice Sourcebook Series, No. 6. New York: Practising Law Institute, 1974.

———. *Successful Labor Relations.* New York: Law Journal Press, 1978.

Levine, Marvin J. *Labor Relations in the Public Sector: Readings and Cases.* 2d ed. Columbus, Ohio: Grid Publishing Company, 1979.

Loevi, Francis J., Jr., and Roger P. Kaplan. *Arbitration and the Federal Sector Advocate: A Practical Guide.* 2d ed. New York: American Arbitration Association, 1982.

McCarthy, Jane, Irving Ladimer, and Josef P. Sirefman. *Managing Faculty Disputes.* San Francisco: Jossey-Bass, Inc., 1984.

McCarthy, Jane, and Irving Ladimer. *Resolving Faculty Disputes.* New York: American Arbitration Association, 1981.

McKelvey, Jean T., ed. *The Changing Law of Fair Representation.* Ithaca: ILR Press, New York State School of Industrial and Labor Relations, Cornell University, 1985.

McPherson, Donald S., Conrad John Gates, and Kevin N. Rogers. *Resolving Grievances: A Practical Approach.* Reston, Va.: Reston Publishing Company, 1983.

Mulcahy, Charles C., and Marion Cartwright Smith. *Last Best Offer: How to Win and Lose. Special Report.* Washington, D.C.: Labor–Management Relations Service of the National League of Cities, United States Conference of Mayors, and National Association of Counties, 1976.

Munro, Robert John. *Grievance Arbitration Procedure: Legal and Policy Guidelines for Public Schools, Community Colleges, and Higher Education.* Tarrytown, N.Y.: Associated Faculty Press, 1982.

Najita, Joyce, and Helene S. Tanimoto. *Interest Disputes Resolution: Final-Offer Arbitration.* Honolulu: University of Hawaii, Industrial Relations Center, 1975.

Nesbitt, Murray B. *Labor Relations in Federal Government Service.* Washington, D.C.: Bureau of National Affairs, 1976.

Nolan, Dennis R. *Labor Arbitration Law and Practice in a Nutshell.* Nutshell Series. St. Paul: West Publishing Company, 1979.

Olson, Gary Scott. *Grievance Arbitration in the Public Schools 1970–1977.* Flagstaff: Northern Arizona University, 1979.

Ostrander, Kenneth H. *A Grievance Arbitration Guide for Educators.* Boston: Allyn and Bacon, 1981.

Pops, Gerald M. *Emergence of the Public Sector Arbitrator.* Lexington, Mass.: Lexington Books, 1976.

————. *Grievance Arbitration in the Public Sector: A Study of Arbitration Decision-Making in New York State.* Ann Arbor, Mich.: Xerox University Microfilms, 1976.

Robinson, James W., Wayne L. Dernoncourt, and Ralph H. Effler. *The Grievance Procedure and Arbitration: Text and Cases.* Washington, D.C.: University Press of America, 1978.

Rynecki, Steven B., and Marvin Hill, Jr. *Preparing and Presenting a Public Sector Grievance Arbitration Case.* Public Employee Relations Library, 58. Washington, D.C.: International Personnel Management Association–United States, 1979.

Savage, Thomas J., and Mark M. Goldstein, comps. *ICLE Seminar Materials for Labor Arbitration.* Newark: Institute for Continuing Legal Education, 1977.

Scheinman, Martin Frank. *Evidence and Proof in Arbitration.* Ithaca: New York State School of Industrial and Labor Relations, Cornell University, 1977.

————. *Expedited Arbitration: Does It Change the Fundamental Jurisprudence of Arbitration?* Master's Thesis. Ithaca: Cornell University, 1976.

Schoen, Sterling H., and Raymond L. Hilgert. *Cases in Collective Bargaining and Industrial Relations: A Decisional Approach.* 5th ed. Homewood, Ill.: Richard D. Irwin, 1986.

Seide, Katherine, ed. *A Dictionary of Arbitration and Its Terms.* Dobbs Ferry, N.Y.: Oceana, 1970.

Somers, Paul C. *An Evaluation of Final Offer Arbitration in Massachusetts.* Personnel and Labor Relations Bulletin, November 1976. Boston: Massachusetts League of Cities and Towns, 1976.

Spitz, John A., ed. *Grievance Arbitration: Techniques and Strategies.* Los Angeles: Institute of Industrial Relations, UCLA, 1977.

Stern, James L., *et al. Final Offer Arbitration: The Effects on Public Safety Employee Bargaining.* Lexington, Mass.: Lexington Books, 1975.

Stone, Morris. *Benefit Plans Disputes: Arbitration Case Stories.* Brookfield, Wis.: International Foundation of Employee Benefit Plans; New York: American Arbitration Association, 1976.

————. *Employee Discipline & Arbitration: Case Stories in Private and Public Employment, with Suggested Questions for Discussion.* New York: American Arbitration Association, 1977.

Stone, Morris, and Earl R. Baderschneider, eds. *Arbitration of Discrimination Grievances.* New York: American Arbitration Association, 1974.

Taylor, Benjamin J., and Fred Witney. *Labor Relations Law.* 5th ed. Englewood Cliffs, N.J.: Prentice-Hall, Inc., 1987.

Tobin, John E. *A Positive Approach to Employee Discipline.* Volume I. Wheaton, Ill.: Hitchcock Publishing Company, 1976.

Trotta, Maurice S. *Arbitration of Labor-Management Disputes.* New York: AMACOM, 1974.

Trower, Chris. *Arbitration at a Glance: A Manual on How to Prepare and Present a Grievance to a Board of Arbitration.* Toronto: Labour Research Institute, 1974.

U.S. Civil Service Commission. Office of Labor-Management Relations. *Grievance Arbitration in the Federal Service: Principles, Practices and Precedents.* Washington, D.C.: 1977.

_____. *Grievance Arbitration in Higher Education: Recent Experience with Arbitration of Faculty Status Disputes.* ACBIS Monograph, no. 6. Washington, D.C.: Academic Collective Bargaining Information Service, 1978.

Werne, Benjamin, ed. *The Law and Practice of Public Employment Labor Relations.* Charlotte: Michie, 1974.

Yaffe, Byron, comp. and ed. *The Saul Wallen Papers: A Neutral's Contribution to Industrial Peace.* Ithaca: New York State School of Industrial and Labor Relations, Cornell University, 1974.

Zack, Arnold M., ed. *Arbitration in Practice.* Ithaca: ILR Press, New York State School of Industrial and Labor Relations, Cornell University, 1984.

_____. *Understanding Fact Finding and Arbitration in the Public Sector.* 3d ed. Washington, D.C.: U.S. Department of Labor, Labor–Management Services Administration, 1980.

_____. *Understanding Grievance Arbitration in the Public Sector.* 3d ed. Washington, D.C.: U.S. Department of Labor, Labor–Management Services Administration, 1980.

Zack, Arnold M., and Richard I. Bloch. *The Arbitration of Discipline Cases: Concepts and Questions.* New York: American Arbitration Association, 1979.

_____. *Labor Agreement in Negotiation and Arbitration.* Washington, D.C.: Bureau of National Affairs, 1983.

## Arbitration Award Services, Conference Proceedings, Periodicals, and Newsletters

*ALRA Newsletter.* Albany: Association of Labor Relations Agencies.

*Arbitration and the Law: AAA General Counsel's Annual Report.* New York: American Arbitration Association.

*Arbitration in the Schools.* New York: American Arbitration Association.

*The Arbitration Journal.* New York: American Arbitration Association.

*Arbitration Times.* New York: American Arbitration Association.

*Daily Labor Report.* Washington, D.C.: Bureau of National Affairs.

*Digest of Labor Arbitration Awards in the Federal Service.* Washington, D.C.: U.S. Civil Service Commission, Office of Labor–Management Relations.

*Employee Relations Law Journal.* New York: Executive Enterprises.

*Federal Employment Relations Manual.* Washington, D.C.: Bureau of National Affairs, 1987.

*The Federal Labor–Management Consultant.* Washington, D.C.: U.S. Civil Service Commission, Office of Labor–Management Relations.

*Federal Labor Relations Reporter* (Vol. 2–Arbitration Awards from the Labor Agreement Information Retrieval System—LAIRS). Fort Washington, Pa.: Labor Relations Press.

*Federal Service Labor Relations Review.* Washington, D.C.: Society of Federal Labor Relations Professionals.

*Government Employee Relations Report.* Washington, D.C.: Bureau of National Affairs.

*Government Union Review.* Vienna, Va.: Public Service Research Foundation.

*Grievance and Discipline Arbitrations.* Albany: New York (State) Office of Employee Relations.

*Industrial and Labor Relations Review.* Ithaca: New York State School of Industrial and Labor Relations, Cornell University.

*Industrial Relations: A Journal of Economy and Society.* Berkeley: Institute of Industrial Relations, University of California.

*Industrial Relations Guide.* Englewood Cliffs, N.J.: Prentice-Hall.

*Industrial Relations Law Journal.* Berkeley: School of Law, University of California at Berkeley.

*Journal of Collective Negotiations in the Public Sector.* Farmingdale, N.Y.: Baywood Publishing Company.

*Journal of Conflict Resolution.* Beverly Hills: Sage Publications.

*LMRS Newsletter.* Washington, D.C.: Labor–Management Relations Service.

*Labor Arbitration Awards.* Chicago: Commerce Clearing House.

*Labor Arbitration in Government.* New York: American Arbitration Association.

*Labor Arbitration Information System.* Fort Washington, Pa.: Labor Relations Press.

*Labor Arbitration Reports.* Washington, D.C.: Bureau of National Affairs.

*Labor Law Journal.* Chicago: Commerce Clearing House.

*Lawyers' Arbitration Letter.* New York: American Arbitration Association.

*The Mediator.* Washington, D.C.: Federal Mediation and Conciliation Service.

*Midwest Monitor: a Digest of Current Literature and Developments in Public Sector Labor Relations.* Bloomington, Ind.: School of Public and Environmental Affairs, Indiana University.

Montana Arbitrators' Association. *Quarterly.* Missoula.

*Monthly Labor Review.* Washington, D.C.: U.S. Bureau of Labor Statistics.

National Academy of Arbitrators. *Proceedings of the Annual Meeting.* Washington, D.C.: Bureau of National Affairs.

*National Public Employment Reporter.* Fort Washington, Pa.: Labor Relations Press; Public Employment Relations Services.

New York University. *Proceedings of the Annual Conference on Labor.* New York: Matthew Bender.

*PERC/IMLR Report.* New Brunswick: Rutgers University, Institute of Management and Labor Relations.

*Public Sector Arbitration Awards.* Minneapolis: Industrial Relations Service Bureau.

*The SFLRP Reporter.* Washington, D.C.: Society of Federal Labor Relations Professionals.

Society of Professionals in Dispute Resolution. *Proceedings of the Annual Meeting.* Washington, D.C.

*SPIDR News.* Washington, D.C.: Society of Professionals in Dispute Resolution.

Southwestern Legal Foundation. *Labor Law Developments: Proceedings of the Annual Institute of Labor Law.* Washington, D.C.: Bureau of National Affairs. Matthew Bender publisher beginning with the 1968 proceedings.

*Steelworkers Arbitration Awards.* Edited by Pike and Fischer. Pittsburgh: United Steelworkers of America.

*Summary of Labor Arbitration Awards.* New York: American Arbitration Association.

*UAW Arbitration Services News Notes.* Indianapolis: United Auto Workers, Arbitration Services Department.

University of Arizona. Institute of Industrial and Labor Relations. *Proceedings of the Annual . . . Labor–Management Conference on Collective Bargaining and Labor Law.* Tucson.

# Code of Professional Responsibility for Arbitrators of Labor–Management Disputes

## Preamble

### BACKGROUND

Voluntary arbitration rests upon the mutual desire of management and labor in each collective bargaining relationship to develop procedures for dispute settlement which meet their own particular needs and obligations. No two voluntary systems, therefore, are likely to be identical in practice. Words used to describe arbitrators (Arbitrator, Umpire, Impartial Chairman, Chairman of Arbitration Board, etc.) may suggest typical approaches but actual differences within any general type of arrangement may be as great as distinctions often made among the several types.

Some arbitration and related procedures, however, are not the product of voluntary agreement. These procedures, primarily but not exclusively applicable in the public sector, sometimes utilize other third party titles (Fact Finder, Impasse Panel, Board of Inquiry, etc.). These procedures range all the way from arbitration prescribed by statute to arrangements substantially indistinguishable from voluntary procedures.

The standards of professional responsibility set forth in this Code are designed to guide the impartial third party serving in these diverse labor–management relationships.

## SCOPE OF CODE

This Code is a privately developed set of standards of professional behavior. It applies to voluntary arbitration of labor–management grievance disputes and of disputes concerning new or revised contract terms. Both "ad hoc" and "permanent" varieties of voluntary arbitration, private and public sector, are included. To the extent relevant in any specific case, it also applies to advisory arbitration, impasse resolution panels, arbitration prescribed by statutes, fact-finding, and other special procedures.

The word "arbitrator," as used hereinafter in the Code, is intended to apply to any impartial person, irrespective of specific title, who serves in a labor–management dispute procedure in which there is conferred authority to decide issues or to make formal recommendations.

The Code is not designed to apply to mediation or conciliation, as distinguished from arbitration, nor to other procedures in which the third party is not authorized in advance to make decisions or recommendations. It does not apply to partisan representatives on tripartite boards. It does not apply to commercial arbitration or to other uses of arbitration outside the labor–management dispute area.

## FORMAT OF CODE

**Bold Face** type, sometimes including explanatory material, is used to set forth general principles. *Italics* are used for amplification of general principles. Ordinary type is used primarily for illustrative or explanatory comment.

## APPLICATION OF CODE

Faithful adherence by an arbitrator to this Code is basic to professional responsibility.

The National Academy of Arbitrators will expect its members to be governed in their professional conduct by this Code and stands ready, through its Committee on Ethics and Grievances, to advise its members as to the Code's interpretation. The American Arbitration Association and the Federal Mediation and Conciliation Service will apply the Code to the arbitrators on their rosters in cases handled under their respective appointment or referral procedures. Other arbitrators and administrative agencies may, of course, voluntarily adopt the Code and be governed by it.

In interpreting the Code and applying it to charges of professional misconduct, under existing or revised procedures of the National Academy of Arbitrators and of the administrative agencies, it should be recognized that while some of its standards express ethical principles basic to the arbitration profession, others rest less on ethics than on considerations of good practice. Experience has shown the difficulty of drawing rigid lines of distinction between ethics and good practice and this Code does not attempt to do so. Rather, it leaves the gravity of alleged misconduct and the extent to which ethical standards have been violated to be assessed in the light of the facts and circumstances of each particular case.

# 1.
# Arbitrator's Qualifications and Reponsibilities to the Profession

## A. GENERAL QUALIFICATIONS

**1. Essential personal qualifications of an arbitrator include honesty, integrity, impartiality and general competence in labor relations matters.**

**An arbitrator must demonstrate ability to exercise these personal qualities faithfully and with good judgment, both in procedural matters and in substantive decisions.**

> a. Selection by mutual agreement of the parties or direct designation by an administrative agency are the effective methods of appraisal of this combination of an individual's potential and performance, rather than the fact of placement on a roster of an administrative agency or membership in a professional association of arbitrators.

**2. An arbitrator must be as ready to rule for one party as for the other on each issue, either in a single case or in a group of cases. Compromise by an arbitrator for the sake of attempting to achieve personal acceptability is unprofessional.**

## B. QUALIFICATIONS FOR SPECIAL CASES

**1. An arbitrator must decline appointment, with-**

**draw, or request technical assistance when he or she decides that a case is beyond his or her competence.**

a. An arbitrator may be qualified generally but not for specialized assignments. Some types of incentive, work standard, job evaluation, welfare program, pension, or insurance cases may require specialized knowledge, experience or competence. Arbitration of contract terms also may require distinctive background and experience.

b. Effective appraisal by an administrative agency or by an arbitrator of the need for special qualifications requires that both parties make known the special nature of the case prior to appointment of the arbitrator.

## C. RESPONSIBILITIES TO THE PROFESSION

**1. An arbitrator must uphold the dignity and integrity of the office and endeavor to provide effective service to the parties.**

a. To this end, an arbitrator should keep current with principles, practices and developments that are relevant to his or her own field of arbitration practice.

**2. An experienced arbitrator should cooperate in the training of new arbitrators.**

**3. An arbitrator must not advertise or solicit arbitration assignments.**

a. It is a matter of personal preference whether an arbitrator includes "Labor Arbitrator" or similar notation on letterheads, cards, or announcements. *It is inappropriate, however, to include memberships or offices held in professional societies or listings on rosters of administrative agencies.*

b. *Information provided for published biographical sketches, as well as that supplied to administrative agencies, must be accurate.* Such information may include membership in professional organizations (including reference to significant offices held), and listings on rosters of administrative agencies.

# 2.
# Responsibilities to the Parties

## A. RECOGNITION OF DIVERSITY IN ARBITRATION ARRANGEMENTS

**1. An arbitrator should conscientiously endeavor to understand and observe, to the extent consistent with professional responsibility, the significant principles governing each arbitration system in which he or she serves.**

a. Recognition of special features of a particular arbitration arrangement can be essential with respect to procedural matters and may influence other aspects of the arbitration process.

**2. Such understanding does not relieve an arbitrator from a corollary responsibility to seek to discern and refuse to lend approval or consent to any collusive**

attempt by the parties to use arbitration for an improper purpose.

## B. REQUIRED DISCLOSURES

1. Before accepting an appointment, an arbitrator must disclose directly or through the administrative agency involved, any current or past managerial, representational, or consultative relationship with any company or union involved in a proceeding in which he or she is being considered for appointment or has been tentatively designated to serve. Disclosure must also be made of any pertinent pecuniary interest.

> a. The duty to disclose includes membership on a Board of Directors, full-time or part-time service as a representative or advocate, consultation work for a fee, current stock or bond ownership (other than mutual fund shares or appropriate trust arrangements) or any other pertinent form of managerial, financial or immediate family interest in the company or union involved.

2. When an arbitrator is serving concurrently as an advocate for or representative of other companies or unions in labor relations matters, or has done so in recent years, he or she must disclose such activities before accepting appointment as an arbitrator.

An arbitrator must disclose such activities to an administrative agency if he or she is on that agency's active roster or seeks placement on a roster. Such disclosure then satisfies this requirement for cases handled under that agency's referral.

a. It is not necessary to disclose names of clients or other specific details. It is necessary to indicate the general nature of the labor relations advocacy or representational work involved, whether for companies or unions or both, and a reasonable approximation of the extent of such activity.

b. *An arbitrator on an administrative agency's roster has a continuing obligation to notify the agency of any significant changes pertinent to this requirement.*

c. When an administrative agency is not involved, an arbitrator must make such disclosure directly unless he or she is certain that both parties to the case are fully aware of such activities.

**3. An arbitrator must not permit personal relationships to affect decision-making.**

**Prior to acceptance of an appointment, an arbitrator must disclose to the parties or to the administrative agency involved any close personal relationship or other circumstance, in addition to those specifically mentioned earlier in this section, which might reasonably raise a question as to the arbitrator's impartiality.**

a. Arbitrators establish personal relationships with many company and union representatives, with fellow arbitrators, and with fellow members of various professional associations. There should be no attempt to be secretive about such friendships or acquaintances but disclosure is not necessary unless some feature of a particular relationship might reasonably appear to impair impartiality.

**4. If the circumstances requiring disclosure are not known to the arbitrator prior to acceptance of appoint-**

ment, disclosure must be made when such circumstances become known to the arbitrator.

5. The burden of disclosure rests on the arbitrator. After appropriate disclosure, the arbitrator may serve if both parties so desire. If the arbitrator believes or perceives that there is a clear conflict of interest, he or she should withdraw, irrespective of the expressed desires of the parties.

## C. PRIVACY OF ARBITRATION

1. All significant aspects of an arbitration proceeding must be treated by the arbitrator as confidential unless this requirement is waived by both parties or disclosure is required or permitted by law.

a. Attendance at hearings by persons not representing the parties or invited by either or both of them should be permitted only when the parties agree or when an applicable law requires or permits. Occasionally, special circumstances may require that an arbitrator rule on such matters as attendance and degree of participation of counsel selected by a grievant.

b. *Discussion of a case at any time by an arbitrator with persons not involved directly should be limited to situations where advance approval or consent of both parties is obtained or where the identity of the parties and details of the case are sufficiently obscured to eliminate any realistic probability of identification.*

A commonly recognized exception is discussion of a problem in a case with a fellow arbitrator. *Any such discussion does not relieve the arbitrator who is acting in the case from sole responsibility for the decision and the discussion must be considered as confidential.*

Discussion of aspects of a case in a classroom without prior specific approval of the parties is not a violation provided the arbitrator is satisfied that there is no breach of essential confidentiality.

c. *It is a violation of professional responsibility for an arbitrator to make public an award without the consent of the parties.*

*An arbitrator may ask the parties whether they consent to the publication of the award either at the hearing or at the time the award is issued.*

(1) *If such question is asked at the hearing it should be asked in writing as follows:*

*"Do you consent to the submission of the award in this matter for publication?*

( )      ( )
YES      NO

*If you consent you have the right to notify the arbitrator within 30 days after the date of the award that you revoke your consent."*

*It is desirable but not required that the arbitrator remind the parties at the time of the issuance of the award of their right to withdraw their consent to publication.*

(2) If the question of consent to the publication of the award is raised at the time the award is issued, the arbitrator may state in writing to each party that failure to answer the inquiry within 30 days will be considered an implied consent to publish.

d. It is not improper for an arbitrator to donate arbitration files to a library of a college, university or similar institution without prior consent of all parties involved. When the circumstances permit, there should be deleted from such donations any cases concerning which one or both of the parties have expressed a desire for privacy. As an additional safeguard, an arbitrator may also decide to withhold recent cases or indicate to the donee a time interval before such cases can be made generally available.

e. *Applicable laws, regulations, or practices of the parties may permit or even require exceptions to the above noted principles of privacy.*

## D. PERSONAL RELATIONSHIPS WITH THE PARTIES

**1. An arbitrator must make every reasonable effort to conform to arrangements required by an administrative agency or mutually desired by the parties regarding communications and personal relationships with the parties.**

a. *Only an "arm's-length" relationship may be acceptable to the parties in some arbitration arrangements or may be required by the rules of an administrative agency. The arbitrator should then have no contact of consequence with representatives of either party while handling a case without the other party's presence or consent.*

b. *In other situations, both parties may want communications and personal relationships to be less formal. It is then appropriate for the arbitrator to respond accordingly.*

## E. JURISDICTION

**1.** An arbitrator must observe faithfully both the limitations and inclusions of the jurisdiction conferred by an agreement or other submission under which he or she serves.

**2.** A direct settlement by the parties of some or all issues in a case, at any stage of the proceedings, must be accepted by the arbitrator as relieving him or her of further jurisdiction over such issues.

## F. MEDIATION BY AN ARBITRATOR

**1.** When the parties wish at the outset to give an arbitrator authority both to mediate and to decide or submit recommendations regarding residual issues, if any, they should so advise the arbitrator prior to appointment. If the appointment is accepted, the arbitrator must perform a mediation role consistent with the circumstances of the case.

    a. Direct appointments, also, may require a dual role as mediator and arbitrator of residual issues. This is most likely to occur in some public sector cases.

**2.** When a request to mediate is first made after appointment, the arbitrator may either accept or decline a mediation role.

    a. *Once arbitration has been invoked, either party*

*normally has a right to insist that the process be continued to decision.*

*b. If one party requests that the arbitrator mediate and the other party objects, the arbitrator should decline the request.*

*c. An arbitrator is not precluded from making a suggestion that he or she mediate. To avoid the possibility of improper pressure, the arbitrator should not so suggest unless it can be discerned that both parties are likely to be receptive. In any event, the arbitrator's suggestion should not be pursued unless both parties readily agree.*

## G. RELIANCE BY AN ARBITRATOR ON OTHER ARBITRATION AWARDS OR ON INDEPENDENT RESEARCH

**1. An arbitrator must assume full personal responsibility for the decision in each case decided.**

*a. The extent, if any, to which an arbitrator properly may rely on precedent, on guidance of other awards, or on independent research is dependent primarily on the policies of the parties on these matters, as expressed in the contract, or other agreement, or at the hearing.*

b. When the mutual desires of the parties are not known or when the parties express differing opinions or policies, the arbitrator may exercise discretion as to these matters, consistent with the acceptance of full personal responsibility for the award.

## H. USE OF ASSISTANTS

**1. An arbitrator must not delegate any decision-making function to another person without consent of the parties.**

>   a. *Without prior consent of the parties, an arbitrator may use the services of an assistant for research, clerical duties, or preliminary drafting under the direction of the arbitrator, which does not involve the delegation of any decision-making function.*

>   b. *If an arbitrator is unable, because of time limitations or other reasons, to handle all decision-making aspects of a case, it is not a violation of professional responsibility to suggest to the parties an allocation of responsibility between the arbitrator and an assistant or associate. The arbitrator must not exert pressure on the parties to accept such a suggestion.*

## I. CONSENT AWARDS

**1. Prior to issuance of an award, the parties may jointly request the arbitrator to include in the award certain agreements between them, concerning some or all of the issues. If the arbitrator believes that a suggested award is proper, fair, sound, and lawful, it is consistent with professional responsibility to adopt it.**

>   a. *Before complying with such a request, an arbitrator must be certain that he or she understands the suggested settlement adequately in order to be able to appraise its terms. If it appears that pertinent facts or circumstances may not have been disclosed, the arbitrator should take the initiative to assure that*

*all significant aspects of the case are fully understood. To this end, the arbitrator may request additional specific information and may question witnesses at a hearing.*

## J. AVOIDANCE OF DELAY

**1. It is a basic professional responsibility of an arbitrator to plan his or her work schedule so that present and future commitments will be fulfilled in a timely manner.**

a. *When planning is upset for reasons beyond the control of the arbitrator, he or she, nevertheless, should exert every reasonable effort to fulfill all commitments. If this is not possible, prompt notice at the arbitrator's initiative should be given to all parties affected. Such notices should include reasonably accurate estimates of any additional time required. To the extent possible, priority should be given to cases in process so that other parties may make alternative arbitration arrangements.*

**2. An arbitrator must cooperate with the parties and with any administrative agency involved in avoiding delays.**

a. *An arbitrator on the active roster of an administrative agency must take the initiative in advising the agency of any scheduling difficulties that he or she can foresee.*

b. *Requests for services, whether received directly or through an administrative agency, should be declined if the arbitrator is unable to schedule a hearing as soon as the parties wish. If the parties, never-theless, jointly desire to obtain the services of the arbitrator and the arbitrator agrees, arrangements should be made by agreement that the arbitrator confidently expects to fulfill.*

c. *An arbitrator may properly seek to persuade the parties to alter or eliminate arbitration procedures or tactics that cause unnecessary delay.*

**3. Once the case record has been closed, an arbitrator must adhere to the time limits for an award, as stipulated in the labor agreement or as provided by regulation of an administrative agency or as otherwise agreed.**

a. *If an appropriate award cannot be rendered within the required time, it is incumbent on the arbitrator to seek an extension of time from the parties.*

b. If the parties have agreed upon abnormally short time limits for an award after a case is closed, the arbitrator should be so advised by the parties or by the administrative agency involved, prior to acceptance of appointment.

## K.   FEES AND EXPENSES

**1. An arbitrator occupies a position of trust in respect to the parties and the administrative agencies. In charging for services and expenses, the arbitrator must be governed by the same high standards of honor and integrity that apply to all other phases of his or her work.**

**An arbitrator must endeavor to keep total charges for services and expenses reasonable and consistent with the nature of the case or cases decided.**

**Prior to appointment, the parties should be aware of or be able readily to determine all significant aspects of an arbitrator's bases for charges for fees and expenses.**

### a. *Services Not Primarily Chargeable on a per Diem Basis*

By agreement with the parties, the financial aspects of many "permanent" arbitration assignments, of some interest disputes, and of some "ad hoc" grievance assignments do not include a per diem fee for services as a primary part of the total understanding. *In such situations, the arbitrator must adhere faithfully to all agreed-upon arrangements governing fees and expenses.*

### b. *Per Diem Basis for Charges for Services*

(1) *When an arbitrator's charges for services are determined primarily by a stipulated per diem fee, the arbitrator should establish in advance his or her bases for application of such per diem fee and for determination of reimbursable expenses.*

*Practices established by an arbitrator should include the basis for charges, if any, for:*

(a) hearing time, including the application of the stipulated basic per diem hearing fee to hearing days of varying lengths;

(b) study time;

(c) necessary travel time when not included in charges for hearing time;

154

(d) postponement or cancellation of hearings by the parties and the circumstances in which such charges will normally be assessed or waived;

(e) office overhead expenses (secretarial, telephone, postage, etc.);

(f) the work of paid assistants or associates.

(2) *Each arbitrator should be guided by the following general principles:*

(a) *Per diem charges for a hearing should not be in excess of actual time spent or allocated for the hearing.*

(b) *Per diem charges for study time should not be in excess of actual time spent.*

(c) *Any fixed ratio of study days to hearing days, not agreed to specifically by the parties, is inconsistent with the per diem method of charges for services.*

(d) *Charges for expenses must not be in excess of actual expenses normally reimbursable and incurred in connection with the case or cases involved.*

(e) *When time or expense are involved for two or more sets of parties on the same day or trip, such time or expense charges should be appropriately prorated.*

(f) *An arbitrator may stipulate in advance a minimum charge for a hearing without violation of (a) or (e) above.*

(3) *An arbitrator on the active roster of an administrative agency must file with the agency his or her individual bases for determination of fees and expenses if the agency so requires. Thereafter, it is*

*the responsibility of each such arbitrator to advise
the agency promptly of any change in any basis for
charges.*

Such filing may be in the form of answers to a
questionnaire devised by an agency or by any other
method adopted by or approved by an agency.

*Having supplied an administrative agency with the
information noted above, an arbitrator's professional
responsibility of disclosure under this Code with
respect to fees and expenses has been satisfied for
cases referred by that agency.*

(4) *If an administrative agency promulgates specific
standards with respect to any of these matters which
are in addition to or more restrictive than an individual arbitrator's standards, an arbitrator on its
active roster must observe the agency standards for
cases handled under the auspices of that agency, or
decline to serve.*

(5) *When an arbitrator is contacted directly by the
parties for a case or cases, the arbitrator has a professional responsibility to respond to questions by
submitting his or her bases for charges for fees and
expenses.*

(6) *When it is known to the arbitrator that one or
both of the parties cannot afford normal charges, it
is consistent with professional responsibility to charge
lesser amounts to both parties or to one of the parties
if the other party is made aware of the difference and
agrees.*

(7) *If an arbitrator concludes that the total of
charges derived from his or her normal basis of cal-
culation is not compatible with the case decided, it*

*is consistent with professional responsibility to charge lesser amounts to both parties.*

**2. An arbitrator must maintain adequate records to support charges for services and expenses and must make an accounting to the parties or to an involved administrative agency on request.**

# 3.
# Responsibilities to Administrative Agencies

## A. GENERAL RESPONSIBILITIES

**1. An arbitrator must be candid, accurate, and fully responsive to an administrative agency concerning his or her qualifications, availability, and all other pertinent matters.**

**2. An arbitrator must observe policies and rules of an administrative agency in cases referred by that agency.**

**3. An arbitrator must not seek to influence an administrative agency by any improper means, including gifts or other inducements to agency personnel.**

> a. It is not improper for a person seeking placement on a roster to request references from individuals having knowledge of the applicant's experience and qualifications.

> b. Arbitrators should recognize that the primary responsibility of an administrative agency is to serve the parties.

# 4.
# Prehearing Conduct

**1. All prehearing matters must be handled in a manner that fosters complete impartiality by the arbitrator.**

a. The primary purpose of prehearing discussions involving the arbitrator is to obtain agreement on procedural matters so that the hearing can proceed without unnecessary obstacles. If differences of opinion should arise during such discussions and, particularly, if such differences appear to impinge on substantive matters, the circumstances will suggest whether the matter can be resolved informally or may require a prehearing conference or, more rarely, a formal preliminary hearing. When an administrative agency handles some or all aspects of the arrangements prior to a hearing, the arbitrator will become involved only if differences of some substance arise.

b. *Copies of any prehearing correspondence between the arbitrator and either party must be made available to both parties.*

# 5.
# Hearing Conduct

## A. GENERAL PRINCIPLES

**1. An arbitrator must provide a fair and adequate**

hearing which assures that both parties have sufficient opportunity to present their respective evidence and argument.

a. *Within the limits of this responsibility, an arbitrator should conform to the various types of hearing procedures desired by the parties.*

b. An arbitrator may: encourage stipulations of fact; restate the substance of issues or arguments to promote or verify understanding; question the parties' representatives or witnesses, when necessary or advisable, to obtain additional pertinent information; and request that the parties submit additional evidence, either at the hearing or by subsequent filing.

c. *An arbitrator should not intrude into a party's presentation so as to prevent that party from putting forward its case fairly and adequately.*

## B. TRANSCRIPTS OR RECORDINGS

**1. Mutual agreement of the parties as to use or non-use of a transcript must be respected by the arbitrator.**

a. *A transcript is the official record of a hearing only when both parties agree to a transcript or an applicable law or regulation so provides.*

b. An arbitrator may seek to persuade the parties to avoid use of a transcript, or to use a transcript if the nature of the case appears to require one. *However, if an arbitrator intends to make his or her appointment to a case contingent on mutual agreement to a transcript, that requirement must be made known to both parties prior to appointment.*

c. If the parties do not agree to a transcript, an arbitrator may permit one party to take a transcript at its own cost. The arbitrator may also make appropriate arrangements under which the other party may have access to a copy, if a copy is provided to the arbitrator.

d. Without prior approval, an arbitrator may seek to use his or her own tape recorder to supplement note taking. The arbitrator should not insist on such a tape recording if either or both parties object.

## C. EX PARTE HEARINGS

**1. In determining whether to conduct an ex parte hearing, an arbitrator must consider relevant legal, contractual, and other pertinent circumstances.**

**2. An arbitrator must be certain, before proceeding ex parte, that the party refusing or failing to attend the hearing has been given adequate notice of the time, place, and purposes of the hearing.**

## D. PLANT VISITS

**1. An arbitrator should comply with a request of any party that he or she visit a work area pertinent to the dispute prior to, during, or after a hearing. An arbitrator may also initiate such a request.**

*a. Procedures for such visits should be agreed to by the parties in consultation with the arbitrator.*

## E. BENCH DECISIONS OR EXPEDITED AWARDS

**1. When an arbitrator understands, prior to accep-**

tance of appointment, that a bench decision is expected at the conclusion of the hearing, the arbitrator must comply with the understanding unless both parties agree otherwise.

a. *If notice of the parties' desire for a bench decision is not given prior to the arbitrator's acceptance of the case, issuance of such a bench decision is discretionary.*

b. *When only one party makes the request and the other objects, the arbitrator should not render a bench decision except under most unusual circumstances.*

**2. When an arbitrator understands, prior to acceptance of appointment, that a concise written award is expected within a stated time period after the hearing, the arbitrator must comply with the understanding unless both parties agree otherwise.**

# 6.
# Post Hearing Conduct

## A. POST HEARING BRIEFS AND SUBMISSIONS

**1. An arbitrator must comply with mutual agreements in respect to the filing or nonfiling of post hearing briefs or submissions.**

a. An arbitrator, in his or her discretion, may either suggest the filing of post hearing briefs or other submissions or suggest that none be filed.

b. When the parties disagree as to the need for briefs, an arbitrator may permit filing but may determine a reasonable time limitation.

**2. An arbitrator must not consider a post hearing brief or submission that has not been provided to the other party.**

## B. DISCLOSURE OF TERMS OF AWARD

**1. An arbitrator must not disclose a prospective award to either party prior to its simultaneous issuance to both parties or explore possible alternative awards unilaterally with one party, unless both parties so agree.**

a. Partisan members of tripartite boards may know prospective terms of an award in advance of its issuance. Similar situations may exist in other less formal arrangements mutually agreed to by the parties. In any such situation, the arbitrator should determine and observe the mutually desired degree of confidentiality.

## C. AWARDS AND OPINIONS

**1. The award should be definite, certain, and as concise as possible.**

a. When an opinion is required, factors to be considered by an arbitrator include: desirability of brevity, consistent with the nature of the case and any expressed desires of the parties; need to use a style and form that is understandable to responsible representatives of the parties, to the grievant and supervisors, and to others in the collective bargaining relationship; necessity of meeting the significant issues; forthrightness to an extent not harmful to the relationship of the parties; and avoidance of gratuitous advice or discourse not essential to disposition of the issues.

## D. CLARIFICATION OR INTERPRETATION OF AWARDS

**1. No clarification or interpretation of an award is permissible without the consent of both parties.**

**2. Under agreements which permit or require clarification or interpretation of an award, an arbitrator must afford both parties an opportunity to be heard.**

## E. ENFORCEMENT OF AWARD

**1. The arbitrator's responsibility does not extend to the enforcement of an award.**

**2. In view of the professional and confidential nature of the arbitration relationship, an arbitrator should not voluntarily participate in legal enforcement proceedings.**

# The United States Arbitration Act

Title 9, U.S. Code, §§ 1–14, was first enacted February 12, 1925 (43 Stat. 883), codified July 30, 1947 (61 Stat. 669), and amended September 3, 1954 (68 Stat. 1233). Chapter 2 was added July 31, 1970 (84 Stat. 692), two new sections 15 were passed by the Congress in October of 1988, and Chapter 3 was added on May 31, 1990.

## Chapter 1.—GENERAL PROVISIONS

§1. "Maritime transactions" and "commerce" defined; exceptions to operation of title

§2. Validity, irrevocability, and enforcement of agreements to arbitrate

§3. Stay of proceedings where issue therein referable to arbitration

§4. Failure to arbitrate under agreement; petition to United States court having jurisdiction for order to compel arbitration; notice and service thereof; hearing and determination

§5. Appointment of arbitrators or umpire

§6. Application heard as motion

§7. Witnesses before arbitrators; fees; compelling attendance

§8. Proceedings begun by libel in admiralty and seizure of vessel or property

§9. Award of arbitrators; confirmation; jurisdiction; procedure

## CHAPTER 1.—GENERAL PROVISIONS

### §1. "Maritime Transactions" and "Commerce" Defined; Exceptions to Operation of Title

"Maritime transaction", as herein defined, means charter parties, bills of lading of water carriers, agreements relating to wharfage, supplies furnished vessels or repairs to vessels, collisions, or any other matters in foreign commerce which, if the subject of controversy, would be embraced within admiralty jurisdiction; "commerce", as herein defined, means commerce among the several States or with foreign nations, or in any Territory of the United States or in the District of Columbia, or between any such Territory and another, or between any such Territory and any State or foreign nation, or between the District of Columbia and any State or Territory or foreign nation, but nothing herein contained shall apply to contracts of employment of seamen, railroad employees, or any other class of workers engaged in foreign or interstate commerce.

## §2. Validity, Irrevocability, and Enforcement of Agreements to Arbitrate

A written provision in any maritime transaction or a contract evidencing a transaction involving commerce to settle by arbitration a controversy thereafter arising out of such contract or transaction, or the refusal to perform the whole or any part thereof, or an agreement in writing to submit to arbitration an existing controversy arising out of such a contract, transaction, or refusal, shall be valid, irrevocable, and enforceable, save upon such grounds as exist at law or in equity for the revocation of any contract.

## §3. Stay of Proceedings Where Issue Therein Referable to Arbitration

If any suit or proceeding be brought in any of the courts of the United States upon any issue referable to arbitration under an agreement in writing for such arbitration, the court in which such suit is pending, upon being satisfied that the issue involved in such suit or proceeding is referable to arbitration under such an agreement, shall on application of one of the parties stay the trial of the action until such arbitration has been had in accordance with the terms of the agreement, providing the applicant for the stay is not in default in proceeding with such arbitration.

## §4. Failure to Arbitrate Under Agreement; Petition to United States Court Having Jurisdiction for Order to Compel Arbitration; Notice and Service Thereof; Hearing and Determination

A party aggrieved by the alleged failure, neglect, or refusal of another to arbitrate under a written agreement for arbitration may petition any United States district court which, save for such agreement, would have jurisdiction under Title 28, in a civil action or in admiralty of the subject matter of a suit arising out of the controversy between the parties, for an order directing that such arbitration proceed in the manner provided for in such agreement. Five days' notice in writing of such application shall be served upon the party in default. Service thereof shall be made in the manner provided by the Federal Rules of Civil Procedure. The court shall hear the parties, and upon being satisfied that the making of the agreement for arbitration or the failure to comply therewith is not in issue, the court shall make an order directing the parties to proceed to arbitration in accordance with the terms of the agreement. The hearing and proceedings, under such agreement, shall be within the district in which the petition for an order directing such arbitration is filed. If the making of the arbitration agreement or the failure, neglect, or refusal to perform the same be in issue, the court shall proceed summarily to the trial thereof. If no jury trial be demanded by the party alleged to be in default, or if the matter in dispute is within admiralty jurisdiction, the court shall hear and determine such issue. Where such an issue is raised, the party alleged to be in default may, except in cases of admiralty, on or before the return day of the notice of application, demand a jury trial of such issue, and upon such demand the court shall make an order referring the issue or issues to a jury in the manner provided by the Federal Rules of Civil Procedure, or may specially call a jury for that purpose. If the jury find that no agreement in writing for arbitration was made or that there is no default in proceeding thereunder, the proceeding shall be dismissed. If the jury find that an agreement for arbitration was made in writing and that there is a default in proceeding thereunder, the court shall make an order summarily directing the parties to proceed with the arbitration in accordance with the terms thereof.

## §5. Appointment of Arbitrators or Umpire

If in the agreement provision be made for a method of naming or appointing an arbitrator or arbitrators or an umpire, such method shall be followed; but if no method be provided therein, or if a method be provided and any party thereto shall fail to avail himself of such method, or if for any other reason there shall be a lapse in the naming of an arbitrator or arbitrators or umpire, or in filling a vacancy, then upon the application of either party to the controversy the court shall designate and appoint an arbitrator or arbitrators or umpire, as the case may require, who shall act under the said agreement with the same force and effect as if he or they had been specifically named therein; and unless otherwise provided in the agreement the arbitration shall be by a single arbitrator.

## §6. Application Heard as Motion

Any application to the court hereunder shall be made and heard in the manner provided by law for the making and hearing of motions, except as otherwise herein expressly provided.

## §7. Witnesses Before Arbitrators; Fees; Compelling Attendance

The arbitrators selected either as prescribed in this title or otherwise, or a majority of them, may summon in writing any person to attend before them or any of them as a witness and in a proper case to bring with him or them any book, record, document, or paper which may be deemed material as evidence in the case. The fees for such attendance shall be the same as the fees of witnesses before masters of the United States courts. Said summons shall issue in the name of the arbitrator or arbitrators, or a majority of them, and shall be signed by the arbitrators, or a majority of them, and shall be directed to the said person and shall be served in the same manner as subpoenas to appear and testify before the court; if any person or persons so summoned to testify shall refuse or neglect to obey said summons, upon petition the United States district court for the district in which such arbitrators, or a majority of them, are sitting may compel the attendance of such person or persons before said arbitrator or arbitrators, or punish said person or persons for contempt in the same manner provided by law for securing the attendance of witnesses or their punishment for neglect or refusal to attend in the courts of the United States.

## §8. Proceedings Begun by Libel in Admiralty and Seizure of Vessel or Property

If the basis of jurisdiction be a cause of action otherwise justiciable in admiralty, then, notwithstanding anything herein to the contrary, the party claiming to be aggrieved may begin his proceeding hereunder by libel and seizure of the vessel or other property of the other party according to the usual course of admiralty proceedings, and the court shall then have jurisdiction to direct the parties to proceed with the arbitration and shall retain jurisdiction to enter its decree upon the award.

## §9. Award of Arbitrators; Confirmation; Jurisdiction; Procedure

If the parties in their agreement have agreed that a judgment of the court shall be entered upon the award made pursuant to the arbitration, and shall specify the court, then at any time within one year after the award is made any party to the arbitration may apply to the court so specified for an order confirming the award, and thereupon the court must grant such an order unless the award is vacated, modified, or corrected as prescribed in sections 10 and 11 of this title. If no court is specified in the agreement of the parties, then such application may be made to the United States court in and for the district within which such award was made. Notice of the application shall be served upon the adverse party, and thereupon the court shall have jurisdiction of such party as though he had appeared generally in the proceeding. If the adverse party is a resident of the district within which the award was made, such service shall be made upon the adverse party or his attorney as prescribed by law for service of notice of motion in an action in the same court. If the adverse party shall be a nonresident, then the notice of the application shall be served by the marshal of any district within which the adverse party may be found in like manner as other process of the court.

## §10. Same; Vacation; Grounds; Rehearing

In either of the following cases the United States court in and for the district wherein the award was made may make an order vacating the award upon the application of any party to the arbitration—

(a)  Where the award was procured by corruption, fraud, or undue means.

(b)  Where there was evident partiality or corruption in the arbitrators, or either of them.

(c)  Where the arbitrators were guilty of misconduct in refusing to postpone the hearing, upon sufficient cause shown, or in refusing to hear evidence pertinent and material to the controversy; or of any other misbehavior by which the rights of any party have been prejudiced.

(d)  Where the arbitrators exceeded their powers, or so imperfectly executed them that a mutual, final, and definite award upon the subject matter submitted was not made.

(e)  Where an award is vacated and the time within which the agreement required the award to be made has not expired the court may, in its discretion, direct a rehearing by the arbitrators.

### §11.  Same; Modification or Correction; Grounds; Order

In either of the following cases the United States court in and for the district wherein the award was made may make an order modifying or correcting the award upon the application of any party to the arbitration—

(a)  Where there was an evident material miscalculation of figures or an evident material mistake in the description of any person, thing, or property referred to in the award.

(b)  Where the arbitrators have awarded upon a matter not submitted to them, unless it is a matter not affecting the merits of the decision upon the matter submitted.

(c)  Where the award is imperfect in matter of form not affecting the merits of the controversy.

The order may modify and correct the award, so as to effect the intent thereof and promote justice between the parties.

## §12. Notice of Motions to Vacate or Modify; Service; Stay of Proceedings

Notice of a motion to vacate, modify, or correct an award must be served upon the adverse party or his attorney within three months after the award is filed or delivered. If the adverse party is a resident of the district within which the award was made, such service shall be made upon the adverse party or his attorney as prescribed by law for service of notice of motion in an action in the same court. If the adverse party shall be a nonresident then the notice of the application shall be served by the marshal of any district within which the adverse party may be found in like manner as other process of the court. For the purposes of the motion any judge who might make an order to stay the proceedings in an action brought in the same court may make an order, to be served with the notice of motion, staying the proceedings of the adverse party to enforce the award.

## §13. Papers Filed with Order on Motions; Judgment; Docketing; Force and Effect; Enforcement

The party moving for an order confirming, modifying, or correcting an award shall, at the time such order is filed with the clerk for the entry of judgment thereon, also file the following papers with the clerk:

(a) The agreement; the selection or appointment, if any, of an additional arbitrator or umpire; and each written extension of the time, if any, within which to make the award.

(b) The award.

(c) Each notice, affidavit, or other paper used upon an application to confirm, modify, or correct the award, and a copy of each order of the court upon such an application.

The judgment shall be docketed as if it was rendered in an action.

The judgment so entered shall have the same force and effect, in all respects, as, and be subject to all the provisions of law relating to, a judgment in an action; and it may be enforced as if it had been rendered in an action in the court in which it is entered.

## §14. Contracts Not Affected

This title shall not apply to contracts made prior to January 1, 1926.

## §15.* Appeals

(a) An appeal may be taken from—
    (1) an order—
        (A) refusing a stay of any action under section 3 of this title,

---

* In 1988, the 100th Congress enacted two laws amending chapter 1 of the U.S. Arbitration Act. One, P.L. 100–702, added a new section 15 providing for appeals. The second, P.L. 100–669, also added a new section 15 concerning the Act of State doctrine. The necessary reconciliation between the conflicting section numbers of these two new laws has not been accomplished as of the date of this publication.

     (B)  denying petition under section 4 of this title to order arbitration to proceed,

     (C)  denying an application under section 206 of this title to compel arbitration,

     (D)  confirming or denying confirmation of an award or partial award, or

     (E)  modifying, correcting, or vacating an award;

  (2)  an interlocutory order granting, continuing, or modifying an injunction against an arbitration that is subject to this title; or

  (3)  a final decision with respect to an arbitration that is subject to this title.

(b)  Except as otherwise provided in section 1292(b) of title 28, an appeal may not be taken from an interlocutory order—

  (1)  granting a stay of any action under section 3 of this title;

  (2)  directing arbitration to proceed under section 4 of this title;

  (3)  compelling arbitration under section 206 of this title; or

  (4)  refusing to enjoin an arbitration that is subject to this title.

## §15. Inapplicability of the Act of State Doctrine

Enforcement of arbitral agreements, confirmation of arbitral awards, and execution upon judgments based on orders confirming such awards shall not be refused on the basis of the Act of State doctrine.

# AAA Offices

**Atlanta (30309-3214) • India Johnson**
1360 Peachtree Street, NE, Suite 270 • (404) 872-3022/881-1134 (Fax)

**Boston (02110-1703) • Richard M. Reilly**
133 Federal Street • (617) 451-6600/451-0763 (Fax)

**Charlotte (28226-8297) • Neil Carmichael**
7301 Carmel Executive Park, Suite 110 • (704) 541-1367/
542-7287 (Fax)

**Chicago (60606-1212) • David Scott Carfello**
205 West Wacker Drive, Suite 1100 • (312) 346-2282/346-0135 (Fax)

**Cincinnati (45202-2809) • Philip S. Thompson**
441 Vine Street, Suite 3308 • (513) 241-8434/241-8437 (Fax)

**Cleveland (44115-1632) • Audrey Mendenhall**
1127 Euclid Avenue, Suite 875 • (216) 241-4741/241-8584 (Fax)

**Dallas (75240-6620) • Helmut O. Wolff**
Two Galleria Tower, Suite 1440 • (214) 702-8222/490-9008 (Fax)

**Denver (80264-2101) • Mark Appel**
1660 Lincoln Street, Suite 2150 • (303) 831-0823/ 832-3626 (Fax)

**Garden City, NY (11530-4789) • Mark A. Resnick**
585 Stewart Avenue, Suite 302 • (516) 222-1660/745-6447 (Fax)

**Hartford (06106-1943) • Karen M. Jalkut**
Two Hartford Square West • (203) 278-5000/246-8442 (Fax)

**Honolulu (96813-4728) • Keith W. Hunter**
810 Richards Street, Suite 641 • (808) 531-0541/533-2306 (Fax)

**Houston (77002-6707) • Therese Tilley**
1001 Fannin Street, Suite 1317 • (713) 739-1302/739-1702 (Fax)

**Kansas City, MO (64106-2110) • Lori A. Madden**
1101 Walnut Street, Suite 903 • (816) 221-6401/471-5264 (Fax)

**Los Angeles (90020-0994) • Jerrold L. Murase**
443 Shatto Place • (213) 383-6516/386-2251 (Fax)

**Miami (33131-2501) • René Grafals**
99 SE Fifth Street, Suite 200 • (305) 358-7777/358-4931 (Fax)

**Michigan (Southfield 48034-7405) • Mary A. Bedikian**
Ten Oak Hollow Street, Suite 170 • (313) 352-5500/352-3147 (Fax)

**Minneapolis (55402-1092) • James R. Deye**
514 Nicollet Mall, Suite 670 • (612) 332-6545/342-2334 (Fax)

**Nashville (37219-2111) • Tony Dalton**
221 Fourth Avenue North • (615) 256-5857/244-8570 (Fax)

**New Jersey (Somerset 08873-4120) • Richard Naimark**
265 Davidson Avenue, Suite 140 • (201) 560-9560/560-8850 (Fax)

**New Orleans (70130-6101) • Deann Gladwell**
650 Poydras Street, Suite 1535 • (504) 522-8781/561-8041 (Fax)

**New York (10020-1203) • Carolyn M. Penna**
140 West 51st Street • (212) 484-4000/307-4387 (Fax)

**Orange County, CA (Irvine 92714-6220) • Lori S. Markowicz**
2601 Main Street, Suite 240 • (714) 474-5090/474-5087 (Fax)

**Orlando (32801-2742) • Mark Sholander**
201 East Pine Street, Suite 800 • (407) 648-1185/649-8668 (Fax)

**Philadelphia (19102-4121) • James L. Marchese**
230 South Broad Street • (215) 732-5260/732-5002 (Fax)

**Phoenix (85012-2803) • Deborah A. Krell**
3033 North Central Avenue, Suite 608 • (602) 234-0950/
    230-2151 (Fax)

**Pittsburgh (15222-1207) • John F. Schano**
Four Gateway Center, Room 419 • (412) 261-3617/261-6055 (Fax)

**St. Louis (63101-1614) • Neil Moldenhauer**
One Mercantile Center, Suite 2512 • (314) 621-7175/621-3730 (Fax)

**Salt Lake City (84111-3834) • Kimberly L. Curtis**
645 South 200 East, Suite 203 • (801) 531-9748

**San Diego (92101-5278) • Dennis Sharp**
525 C Street, Suite 400 • (619) 239-3051/239-3807 (Fax)

**San Francisco (94104-1113) • Charles A. Cooper**
417 Montgomery Street • (415) 981-3901/781-8426 (Fax)

**Seattle (98104-1455) • Neal M. Blacker**
811 First Avenue, Suite 200 • (206) 622-6435/343-5679 (Fax)

**Syracuse (13202-1376) • Deborah A. Brown**
205 South Salina Street • (315) 472-5483/472-0966 (Fax)

**Washington, DC (20036-3169) • Garylee Cox**
1730 Rhode Island Avenue, NW, Suite 509 • (202) 296-8510/
    872-9574 (Fax)

**White Plains, NY (10601-4485) • Marion J. Zinman**
34 South Broadway • (914) 946-1119/946-2661 (Fax)